Respecting Your Piers

A comedy

Peter Quilter

Samuel French — Londc
New York - Toronto - Hollywoo

GW00771950

© 2000 BY PETER QUILTER

RESPECTING YOUR PIERS

First produced by Gut Reaction Theatre Company in the autumn of 1994 on a national tour. The commissioning of the play was part-funded by a grant from the Arts Council of Great Britain.

The premiére took place at the Roses Theatre in Tewkesbury on 17th September, 1994, with the following cast:

Sharon	Joh Smith
Theresa	Catherine Ellerman
Pam	Teresa Selfe
Betty	Norma Howard
Jackie	Wendy Young

Produced by **Jack Milner** and **Debby Holden**
Directed by **Mike Burnside**
Designed by **Gerri Livesey**

The sixty-venue tour ended at The Players Theatre in London.

CHARACTERS

Theresa, plain in appearance, mid/late 20s
Sharon, a full-figured gothic punk, 20s
Pam, Theresa's embittered mother
Betty, Theresa's lively grandmother
Jackie, slim, sporty, well-dressed, late 30s

The action of the play takes place on a seaside pier

Time: the present

AUTHOR'S NOTE

In Act II, the actress playing the character of Pam has to dress up to vaguely resemble a famous singing star. Who this singing star is will be up to the company putting on the show. It is my suggestion that you select a well-known singing celebrity who is instantly recognizable in terms of what she looks like and the kind of clothes she wears. Your selected celebrity should be of a similar build and age group to your actress, and one that makes regular appearances in the UK. There are many points in the script where the chosen celebrity's name needs to be inserted into the dialogue. These read something like this:

What's all this about [CELEBRITY]?

You will also need to select songs from the celebrity's repertoire. A couple of these are used for little moments of singing by characters. A third song is used in the "concert" sequence. Although Pam does not actually get to sing, you will need a karaoke-style backing track for this concert song. The choices for your celebrity are many and varied—and I hope you have fun choosing one!

P.Q.

(Please read the PRS notice on page viii in regard to any music used)

Dedication

Peter Quilter would like to dedicate this play
to the following people:

Margaret Florence Quilter (his mum)

Beatrice Quilter (his nan)
who inspired the character of Betty

Claire Nelson (his friend)
who inspired the character of Sharon

and

Aunty Dawn

ACT I

SCENE 1

An office at the entrance of a pleasure pier

The office contains basic tables, chairs and filing cabinets, plus a scattering of material from the pier—a broken deck-chair, a poster for the end-of-pier theatre, assorted boxes and crates. The office also houses the pier's radio station which is signified only by a tatty sign hanging above a turntable, speakers and stacks of seven inch records

As the CURTAINS *rise, the stage is in darkness. Wurlitzer organ music plays—* I Do Like to Be Beside the Seaside. *After a while, the music begins to fade down, ideally giving the impression that it is disappearing into the distance. As this happens, the Lights very slowly come up on the dilapidated pier office, which is strewn with litter and dust. Several cardboard boxes are stacked up by the door. The pier itself can be seen through the windows stretching off into the distance*

When the music has faded out completely, the door is pushed open by Theresa and the boxes tumble to the floor

She enters and clears the boxes to one side. She collects some bags of shopping from just outside the door and places them on the table. She then looks around for a few moments. She finds an old book lying in a corner and opens it up. She blows the dust from the pages and is engulfed by a cloud of debris. She coughs violently

Pam enters

Pam Oh, charming!
Theresa It's very dusty.
Pam I gathered. I'll leave the door open. (*She wedges the door open*) I had no idea it would be in this state.
Theresa It has been quite a few years.
Pam Even so.
Theresa I'll make a cup of tea, shall I?

Pam Are you sure it's hygienic? I could do without termites in my PG Tips this morning.

Theresa I can promise you that won't happen—I didn't bring PG Tips. (*She starts unpacking her bags. She brings out biscuits and two stacks of Max Pax instant cup drinks*)

Pam What on earth have you got there?

Theresa Max Pax. I found them at the back of the cupboard.

Pam What cupboard?

Theresa The blue door cupboard, in your kitchen.

Pam Oh, for Heaven's sake, you shouldn't be rooting around back there— God knows what you'll come across.

Theresa Well, I found these. And they're still within their use-by date.

Pam Which is?

Theresa Two thousand and twenty.

Pam Oh, good. So long as I get my week's supply of preservative. How many have you got?

Theresa Twelve Tea and twelve Coffee. (*She produces a kettle from another bag and a couple of plates. She fills the kettle from a plastic bottle of filtered water as the conversation continues*)

Pam That should be plenty. There's only Sharon and your Nan isn't there.

Theresa Yes.

Pam Nobody else?

Theresa No, Mum. Not today. You've already asked me that.

Pam Just making sure.

Theresa prepares to plug the kettle into a socket

Careful with that.

Theresa It'll be fine. The generator was checked this week.

Pam I've heard that one before. Just keep your rubber soles on the floor.

Theresa plugs in the kettle, switches it on, and tops it up with water

Theresa Do you want to fetch Nan?

Pam Give her a few more minutes, she wanted to have a snooze.

Theresa How does she feel about all this? Have you talked to her about it?

Pam I gave her the basics, that's all. I called in after the reading of the will. "Hallo, Mum", I said, "Get the whisky out of the pantry, your son's just left you a pleasure pier".

Theresa Oh, Mum!

Pam Well what else am I supposed to say? Better to come right out with it.

Theresa What was her reaction?

Pam Erm… "Silly bugger" I think were the exact words. I don't think she understood that the pier was Michael's to give away. She knew he'd inherited it from his uncle, but she hadn't seen that brother in years, so... All in all, it was a lot for her to take in. Your brother dies, then your son dies as well, all of a sudden. It's been hard for all of us, but you can imagine what she had to get through.

Theresa She doesn't show it, though, does she?

Pam She's slowed down a bit. But that'll pass. Give her a month or two and she'll be charging about like a twelve-year-old as usual.

Theresa Do you want to sit down?

Pam I'm a bit frightened to.

Theresa wipes the dust from a chair and Pam sits. Pam looks around

What a bloody mess.

Theresa I don't think it's too bad. A quick wipe, chuck some of it out. We'll have it sorted out in no time.

Pam Yes, we ought to do something. We're going to need somewhere to sit around and talk everything through. Did you bring all the papers?

Theresa Yes.

Pam Have you read them through again? You said you were going to.

Theresa I had a go. The basic premise of it is clear enough, but all the legal jargon is a bit mind-numbing.

Pam For you? Why? You went to university.

Theresa Well, yes——

Pam "Well, yes"—four hundred pounds a term "yes", thank you very much. Whenever anything complicated turns up, you can't help. I don't know why we bothered.

Theresa I didn't read law, Mum.

Pam No, but you read English, Theresa—and the documents are in English, aren't they? Or did they translate them into Arabic just to be difficult?

Theresa It's just very convoluted. A bit beyond me.

Pam I don't know. Three years at Kent University and all you came back with was a certificate, a square hat and a middle-class accent.

Theresa Mother, will you stop being horrible.

Pam So long as you can explain things properly to Mum and to Sharon. If they're as stunned as I am, they'll need it to be gone over again and again.

Theresa I think they'll be fine. They've got the general idea. It's the sharing of ownership that needs to be talked about, there are all sorts of entanglements.

Pam Entangle...? Could we avoid all these big words for this morning. Plain English will be fine.

Theresa Just showing you my three years at uni weren't a complete waste.

Pam Anyway, there aren't any entanglements, are there? It's a straight split, there's no more to it than that.

Theresa Put simply, yes, but—well, that's why we're here, isn't it? To iron out all the little details.

Pam And to decide what to do. It's all such a silly way to go about things. But that was your father. Never the easy way through anything. Are those drinks ready?

Theresa It's still boiling.

Pam I can't see how it can work. Five women owning equal shares in a pier. And look at the place!

Theresa It's all he had to give us. It meant so much to him.

Pam You think so?

Theresa Oh, yes. He loved this pier. He spent his childhood here with his uncle. You know how often he talked about it. And when I came down here as a little girl, he used to tell me all these stories. And when Great Uncle Bill left him the pier, I thought it was just the most wonderful thing. Perfect. But Dad never got to enjoy it. That's the saddest thing. Things happened so quickly, he never even got to come down here.

Pam You can blame the lawyers for that. It took them so bloody long to verify Bill's will.

Theresa It's tragic, isn't it? But now it's ours. He had this precious thing that he couldn't enjoy, and so he gave it to his five favourite people.

Pam "Favourite"? No, dear, I don't think I was among his favourites.

Theresa He never hated you. I never heard Dad say anything like that.

Pam He didn't need to say anything, did he? Walking out the front door with a suitcase says it all, doesn't it!

Theresa Whatever it was all about, he wanted to give something to each of the five of us. And I think it's lovely. (*She switches the kettle off*)

Pam I'm not saying it wasn't thoughtful. It's just strange, that's all—forcing me and that woman into any kind of deal.

Theresa Well, she's not here today, so you don't have to worry about it just yet, do you? You want tea, I presume.

Pam Yes, but check in the bottom of the cup for droppings before you put the water in.

Sharon peers through the open door

Sharon Anybody home!?
Theresa Sharon! Hi! Come in.

Sharon comes in. She wears outrageous leather/punk/gothic clothes and spectacular brightly coloured hair which shoots off in all directions. Theresa and Sharon hug. A handshake from Pam

Pam Very punctual.

Sharon Yes, very good going for me. Couldn't wait to see the place, actually. Now that I own a fifth of it.

Theresa Have you been here before?

Sharon Not since I was three foot high. Looks much as I remember it, though … shabby and covered in crap.

Theresa It's all a bit of a shock, isn't it?

Sharon Michael never let on about this to me—not a dickybird. I didn't really expect anything at all, let alone twenty per cent of a Helter Skelter and a Bingo Parlour! When I told my boyfriend Stevey about it, he went hysterical. Brought on his asthma.

Theresa He never was a very predictable man, my father. But even so...

Sharon My very own pleasure pier, eh? That'll show those squatters at number twenty-six. Though I'm not so keen on the idea of having to run the place. Fifty words a minute I can cope with, but selling cockles is beyond me. (*She looks round. Sarcastically*) Are all the buildings as glamorous and tidy as this?

Theresa Most of them.

Pam (*to Sharon*) You hair's changed colour, hasn't it?

Sharon Since the last time I saw you, yes. On the day of the funeral, I had it done green. Sort of a tribute.

Pam I'm sure he appreciated that.

Sharon It's a bit of a mess at the moment. I've been putting Camomile in it to try and make it go blonde, but it doesn't seem to be working.

Theresa Can I get you a drink?

Sharon Please. (*She sees the Max Pax*) Broke into a vending machine then?

Theresa No, I brought these this morning. Thought it would make things more efficient. Tea or coffee?

Sharon Black tea, please.

Theresa (*examining Max Pax*) Sorry, I can only do white tea with sugar.

Sharon Oh. What's the coffee?

Theresa White with no sugar.

Sharon I'll have the coffee.

Theresa (*making the drinks*) How is Stevey?

Sharon Fine. Been with him two years now. Two and a half if you count the period when he was in the detention centre... He was caught stealing toys for Children in Need. He loves his charity work.

Pam Well, I think I'd better go and collect your Nan. (*To Sharon*) I thought it best she stayed in the car while we got the room tidied up and the kettle on.

Sharon Oh, right. There's a load of them sat in cars along the front. It's like a rally. All sat staring into space and sucking on sweets. There was one in a red Metro with a face like sin.

Pam Yes, that's her. (*She makes for the exit*) Won't be a mo'.

Pam exits

Sharon Whoops…

Theresa Don't worry. Help yourself to biscuits. (*She offers over a couple of packets*)

Sharon Can I have a look at the calories? (*She reads the panels*) These are a bit less. (*She picks one of the less calorific ones*) What about Jackie? She here?

Theresa She's busy today with a marketing job. She'll join us later on in the week.

Sharon What are things like between her and your mum?

Theresa Not great. Mum has never forgiven Dad for leaving, and she's always blamed Jackie for what happened. They're not the best of friends.

Sharon Not surprising, really. If I was shagging your bloke, we wouldn't exactly be best chums either.

Theresa That is one way of putting it… Not that I have a "bloke"—or any prospects of getting one at the moment.

Sharon Still single?

Theresa Afraid so—and hurtling towards thirty.

Sharon (*taking another biscuit*) You'll get someone soon, don't you worry. Cupid will hurl a grenade in your direction. You shouldn't have any problem now that you're eligible—you know, joint owner of a pleasure pier—very sexy.

Theresa You think so?

Sharon Oh yes, all that power and influence—and free tickets for the Bingo. Essex Man will be on to you like a shot.

Theresa I'm not sure Essex Man is quite what I'm after.

Sharon Well, beggars can't be choosers… Think I'll try one of these ones. (*She takes one of the other packets of biscuits*) Shouldn't be eating biscuits at all, really. Very bad for you.

Theresa brings Sharon a cup of instant white coffee and sits down with her own cup of Max Pax

Cheers. (*She drinks*) Ergh—tastes like warmed-up sick.

Theresa Oh. Shall I make you something else?

Sharon No, I quite like it. (*She starts wandering around the office, investigating everything and playing with things*) This the main office, is it?

Theresa Seems to be where everything is. That's where they did the Pier Radio from, (*she gestures*) in the corner, and all the paperwork seems to be in these filing cabinets.

Sharon All we need now is an underground bunker for when your mum and Jackie declare war on each other.

Theresa I don't think it will be that bad. I hope not. Just keep your fingers crossed.

Sharon Well, at the end of the day we have to make it work, don't we—we have to work together somehow. I mean, that's the deal, isn't it? (*She takes and consumes another biscuit*) That's the way the cookie crumbles...

Theresa Have you not had lunch?

Sharon No, I'm skipping lunches this week—part of the diet.

Theresa You don't look like you need to lose weight to me.

Sharon Ah, but it depends who you compare yourself with, though, doesn't it? I mean, in comparison with Pavarotti I look fine, but put me next to Joanna Lumley and it'll look like she's hanging round with a punk elephant!

Theresa Yes, but how often are you going to find yourself standing next to Joanna Lumley?

Sharon You never know—I go to a lot of car boot sales... (*She explains*) You always get a celebrity or two at them. These rich people love a bargain. Stevey loves markets and that—he'll barter over something for hours and hours—before he finally nicks it. He'll come over here in a few days—help with all the manual stuff that needs doing.

Theresa There'll be plenty of that. It's all in a pretty bad state. Come on, let's start cleaning this place up a bit. (*She proceeds to clean and tidy the office*)

Sharon just keeps investigating things

I'd love to properly preserve this place. People don't see these piers as part of our history, but I do. The past is written right through them.

Sharon Just like sticks of rock.

Theresa Um?

Sharon Stuff written right through it.

Theresa Oh, yes, I see what you mean.

Sharon Did you come here a lot when you were a sprog?

Theresa A Sprog? I don't think I was ever a Sprog. I was a Brownie for a while.

Sharon A child, I mean, when you were little. With Michael, you know—did your Dad bring you here as a kid?

Theresa Oh, yes, all the time. (*She stops clearing*) All the big weekends. Birthdays, holidays. I'd rush through the gate. Hot doughnut first, then straight to the Ghost Train. It's brilliant—there's a slide in the middle that you whizz down and two big doors at the top where you come outside for a few seconds before crashing back into the darkness—and then whoosh down the slide again. And all those terrible luminous dummies and kaleidoscope effects, cobwebs, spiders, skeletons ... whoosh! Whoosh!

A pause

Sharon (*drily*) Sounds thrilling.

Theresa I just used to scream my head off. I wasn't scared or anything; I just liked screaming my head off.

Sharon I bet you were a real live wire! Did Michael come on the rides with you?

Theresa Always. It was just us two, in the little car. Him hugging me really tightly. Me feeling scared, but protected. And excited by the ride—all these feelings at the same time. It was great. All the bright lights running over your head, the silly dummies making you laugh and laugh. Down the slide, your stomach turning. Dad laughing. Clinging on to him. His arm round my shoulders… It was at times like that I really felt close to him… I really miss him…

Silence for a moment

Sharon Have some chocolate. (*She takes a bar of chocolate out of her pocket*)

They both eat

I wish I had brought Stevey, now. He might help cheer things up… We could find him a proper job here, couldn't we? He's hopelessly unemployed. It's crazy. We've got so many debts. Some money from this place would really sort us out. Stevey would be handy, wouldn't he?

Theresa Oh, yes. If we all agree to get the pier up and running, we'll need all sorts of people working here, selling tickets, bingo calling, operating the rides.

Sharon He could do that—he's very good with the public.

Theresa Yes. Though, he'd have to have a uniform and cover his tattoos. When families come for a day out, they don't really want to read "vomit" on someone's forehead. But I'm sure we can find something for him.

Sharon You could station him at the end of the Ghost Train. The cars would come out of the tunnel with people relieved that the ride was over, then they'd look up and see Stevey—and scream their tits off!

They both laugh

Pam and Betty enter the office from outside

Pam Well, here we are. (*To Sharon*) Do you know Michael's mother?

Sharon Not really.

Pam This is Betty. (*To Betty*) This is Sharon, Nan, she was Michael's secretary.

Sharon Um, assistant.

Sharon and Betty shake hands

Nice to meet you, Betty.
Theresa You all right, Nan?
Betty Yes, dear, thank you.
Theresa What do you want to drink?
Pam Coffee for me. Do you want a drink, Nan?
Betty Hot chocolate.
Theresa Can't do it, sorry. Just tea or coffee.
Betty Oh... Tea.
Theresa It's white with one sugar, is that all right?

Betty looks bemused. Theresa makes the drinks

Biscuits are over there. There's Rich Tea and Chocolate Digestives. The Rich Tea are lower in calories, apparently.
Sharon I suppose I could have one more. (*She takes a biscuit*)
Pam (*to Betty*) Do you want a biscuit?
Betty What are they, Ginger Snaps?
Pam Digestives.
Betty No, thank you. Not for me. (*She takes a biscuit*)
Pam Sit down, Nan, take it easy.

Betty sits

She's still a bit taken aback by it all. Wake up one morning and find yourself the owner of a pleasure pier. Not the sort of surprise any of us are used to.
Sharon You're telling me. I'm dead excited, though. I think it'll be a real adventure. Great fun.
Pam Fun!? Well ... possibly. Though I wouldn't hope for an easy ride with that girlfriend of his involved—her with the face-lift and the lycra body stockings.
Theresa She doesn't wear body stockings.
Pam Have you not seen her in them? Looks like four pound of pork chops in a three pound bag.
Sharon How long ago did you and Michael split up?
Pam Several years. While Theresa was at university. Her dad was trying to catch his lost youth with Jackie. One of several things I imagine you could catch off of her.
Betty Michael was an idiot. Don't know where he gets it from... Mind you,

he's always been the same, you never knew where you were with him. He was never very bright, you know, not if I'm honest about it. I told him so and all. His brother was out there doing all these exams, all these examinations. But not Michael.

Pam What do you mean? Michael went to college.

Betty Not like his brother did. His brother went to lots of them.

Pam That's because they kept throwing him out!

Betty His brother Robert was smart. That's why they didn't get on too well. Robert was a clever boy, much brighter than Michael, God rest his soul. And look at his brother now; comfortable, plenty of money—and with the same wife he started out with.

Pam Here we go…

Betty You don't run off with some … Marks and Spencer's type, just like that. People changing wives these days like they're trying out a new supermarket. Don't know what he saw in Marks and Spencer's. (*With a thumb towards Pam*) Should have stuck to Asda.

Pam Oh, thank you!

Betty Well… Where's me hot chocolate?

Theresa It's tea. Just tea or coffee. I made you tea. White with one sugar.

Betty He was an idiot. I always told him so.

Pam All right now, that's enough—you'll get upset.

Betty I won't! I won't get upset! Can't afford to—not on a pension.

Theresa All right, let's all calm down—can we? Please? The least you can do is give Jackie a fair chance. I'm sure once she's here we'll be able to settle down and forget all this. You'll feel fine once Jackie's actually here. Won't you, Mum?

Complete silence

Sharon (*jumping in to change the subject*) Those beams are in a state, aren't they!? Under the pier. The beams. Rotting away.

Theresa Yes, Sharon, there really is a lot of work needed.

Pam It's impossible, if you ask me. It needs a thorough clean, major re-decoration, half the mechanics don't work any more; Andy Pandy's Merry-Go-Round is a death trap. And all this before we could even set about running the place. Doomed to failure. It's like being a passenger on the Titanic.

Theresa I'm sure we can do it, if we all pull together.

Pam Have you ever tried to raise half a million pounds?

Theresa No. But that's part of the challenge, isn't it?

Pam shakes her head in despair

We have to try, Mum! We can't give up hope on our first day!

Sharon I agree. We have to give it a good shot. I for one am not missing out on a chance for some dosh. We can get on with raising money and, meanwhile, try to get everything cleared up and mended. It's amazing what you can do when you just try. Come on, I'll have a crack at this thing for starters. (*She goes over to the radio*)
Theresa What?
Sharon The radio. It's supposed to still work, is it?
Theresa Should do.
Sharon Well, then, let's start as we mean to go on—get the old thing going.
Theresa Do you know about electrics?
Sharon That and hairdressing are my two strong points.
Theresa You sure you know what you're doing?
Sharon It's bound to be obvious. (*She looks over the radio set-up*)
Theresa And is it?
Sharon No, not really... (*She flicks a random switch*)

There is a thump and a high pitched squeal from the speakers, which are set up directly behind Betty's head. Theresa covers her ears, Pam's face registers great pain and Betty jumps up in shock throwing her tea everywhere

I think we got something there.
Theresa Yes, our first floor stain. I'll get a cloth. You all right, Nan?
Betty It's like being back in the war round here.
Pam Turn the volume down, you don't want to blow the speakers.
Sharon I haven't found the volume yet. Oh, here it is. (*She adjusts a control*) Sorry about that. Right then, do you want to hear something?
Theresa (*cleaning up the spilt tea*) Are the tapes all there?
Sharon No tapes. It's all records. Singles.
Pam They look very dusty.
Sharon No worse than the rest of the place. (*She blows an inch of dust off one*) Here we go. (*She cleans the record on her sleeve and puts it on to play*)

Suddenly, we hear blasting out the opening chords of some horrendous heavy metal record. Sharon head-bangs to the music. The record plays normally for a few moments, then jumps a few lines, jumps back again, sticks on a word, screeches across the vinyl, sticks again, scratches, shudders, screeches, then cuts off in mid sentence turning itself off with a loud bang

Pam Yes, it really is amazing what you can achieve when you just try.
Sharon Just a slight technical hitch. I'll have another go after lunch. Better still—I'll let Stevey have a look at it. He's a real whizz at electrics. He's got a City in Guilds Diploma.
Theresa In electrics?

Sharon No, catering—but it's much the same thing.

Theresa I'm sure we'll find Stevey very useful to have around.

Pam Yes, if we run low on cash, he can rob some banks for us! … Sorry, Sharon, I didn't mean to be quite so offensive.

Sharon No, I'll mention it to him.

Theresa Perhaps we could put on a big fund-raising concert? See if we can persuade some celebrities to come along.

Sharon Good idea. Got anyone in mind?

Theresa Not really.

Betty What about [CELEBRITY]?

Sharon Oh yes, Betty, that's a great idea. We could maybe give her a ring— I mean it is a good cause, isn't it?

Theresa Yes, it's a wonderful cause. Though I don't think we should get our hopes up—she must always be terribly busy. But everything's worth a try.

Sharon Does the theatre work?

Theresa Oh, yes. The Operatic Society still put shows on. It's quite big as well.

Pam Just a moment. We haven't agreed we're going to do anything yet. Doesn't anyone think it would just be better all round if we sell the place for scrap?

Theresa What scrap? Nobody wants an old pier. Besides, I'd never agree to it. I want to save the pier, not destroy it. I thought we'd agreed on this!?

Pam Just thought it was worth mentioning again. I mean, we're not even all here, are we?

Theresa I've spoken to Jackie and she wants the same as me. Dad put his faith in us to do this for him and Jackie has no intention of letting him down.

Pam Fine. Just don't say I didn't warn you. Come on, then, we might as well get on with it.

Theresa Right.

Pam Important things first.

Theresa (*picking the papers up*) The documents?

Pam No, Theresa; to use one of your big words—lubrication.

Sharon Lubrication?

Pam Yes. Cup of tea! Put the kettle back on.

Sharon Oh, tea! When you said "lubrication" I thought you meant——

Pam Yes, I can imagine what you thought. Have another biscuit.

Sharon eats a biscuit, as Theresa puts the kettle back on, as Pam stares at Sharon with a look of mild horror

Black-out. Music

SCENE 2

A sign above the stage is caught by a spotlight. It reads "Two Days Later".
It is morning

When the Lights come up, we see the office has been tidied up, boxes removed
and litter cleared. A rusty automated bingo machine that randomly selects
numbered balls stands C

Theresa is trying to turn it on, as Pam watches

Theresa Oh, bother. It's not working.
Pam Something else that needs mending—all this is getting to be very
   expensive.
Theresa Well, you're the one that's agreed to deal with all the money. I'll
   leave it with you to decide what's best.

   Betty enters

Betty What's all this then?
Pam It's not working.
Betty Oh, dear. That's a shame... What isn't working?
Pam The bingo thing.
Betty Eh?
Theresa An automatic caller. Picks the numbers for you. For bingo.
Betty What do you want a machine to do that for? People come to play bingo,
   don't want a machine. They want a human up there giving out numbers,
   a friendly face.
Theresa You still have a caller, Nan. This just picks the balls out for them.
Betty Picks the balls out? Stupid. Here, let me have a go. (*She opens up the*
   lid and puts her hand into the machine. She pulls a ball out) Here we are,
   easy. No electrics or anything. (*She looks at the ball*) Legs Eleven.
Pam What?
Betty That's what they say—number eleven. Couple of Legs. (*She picks out*
   another) All the Threes—thirty-three. (*She picks out another*) Blind
   Forty—no, Fifty. Blind Twenty. (*She looks closer*) Oh, bugger. (*She puts*
   it back, gets another) On Its Own... Thirty-seven. (*She picks out another*
   ball) Two Fat Ladies—forty-one.
Theresa Isn't it normally a young chap that does the calling in places like
   this?
Pam Oh, I see, looking for romance, are we?
Theresa No, of course not.
Betty Kelly's Eye. (*She squints at the ball*) Three hundred and seventy.

Pam Well, Betty seems to have finally found her vocation in life.
Betty All the sixes ... no, sevens. Is that a seven or a four? (*She gives the ball to Theresa*)
Theresa (*examining the ball*) It's a golf ball, Nan.
Betty That shouldn't be in there. (*To Pam*) Should it?
Pam I don't know. The cut-throat world of bingo isn't really my thing.

Sharon enters

Sharon Hey, bingo time! Brilliant! Excellent!
Pam The machine doesn't work.
Sharon Oh. Well, so much for that short burst of excitement. Any news on [CELEBRITY]?
Theresa I sent a fax to her agent.
Sharon Did you? Well that sounds promising.
Theresa Not at all. I only did it for fun, really. Is Stevey with you?
Sharon No, he's still at home working on his moped. I got a lift from Jackie.

Pam nearly dies of shock

Pam Jackie!? You mean she's here? Is she here?
Sharon Oh, yeah. She's just finding a parking space.
Pam Oh, my God...
Betty Here we go, here we go...
Theresa I do hope you're going to be friendly, Mum.
Pam I wouldn't hope for too much, darling.
Theresa At least make an effort. We are all in this together, we do have to try and get on.

There is a knock on the door

Jackie (*off*) Hallo! Anybody home?
Theresa Yes, Jackie, we're in here. Come in.

Jackie enters, dressed in the latest fashionable sportswear

Jackie Oh, this is nice. Hallo. (*She sees the bingo machine*) What's that?
Betty It selects balls.
Jackie Really? Hallo, Betty, how are you?
Betty Not so bad.
Jackie (*with a nod*) Pam.

A cursory nod from Pam. Jackie gives Theresa a kiss

How's it all going?

Theresa Fine. Fine.

Jackie Good. I got the message about the paint. It's all in the boot of the Astra—I picked the colours out myself.

Theresa That's great, thank you.

Jackie I picked up some brushes and rollers while I was there—so we can all get painting this afternoon. I've got the receipts here. (*She produces a couple of receipts*)

Theresa You need to give those to Mum, she's dealing with all that. Sort of a Treasurer, aren't you, Mum?

Pam snatches the receipts from Jackie's hands

Pam Sort of. (*Desperate to get away*) Well—I'll go and fetch those things then.

Theresa What things?

Pam The things. Things for the—for the thing. Are you coming, Nan? To help with the—with the things?

Betty What things?

Pam (*aggressive*) Are you coming or staying?

Betty I'll come, dear.

Pam Right. See you all later.

Pam exits quickly

Betty slowly follows behind

Betty (*as though to explain*) Menopause.

Betty exits

Theresa I'm sorry about that, Jackie.

Jackie It's all right. No, really, it is. I'm used to it by now. Our paths cross quite often, really. Just a few weeks ago, in fact. At Sainsbury's. I was at the salads and Pam was queuing up for a cheese sandwich and a Mars Bar. Her eyes glared at me like a furnace. Then she marched off. What can you do? You just have to carry on.

Sharon But how will you manage? We're going to have to work so closely together.

Jackie The first few days are always the worst. It will get better. Anyway, how are you?

Theresa I'm fine. I've been a bit down. But this place has really perked me up.

Jackie You like it?

Theresa I love it. I think it's just wonderful. So old and majestic. I really hope we can make this work.

Jackie I'll certainly do all I can. Why Michael went about it all like this, I just don't know. He did have a wicked sense of humour. But if it's what he wanted as his legacy, then that's fine. I just wish he hadn't made it so complicated... I brought a costume with me—a giant teddy bear.

Theresa Oh?

Jackie I thought it might be useful for advertising. Someone could dress up in it and give out leaflets or something. We use them at supermarket openings and events like that. (*She pulls a large cardboard box into view from just outside the door. She takes out a giant fur body costume and a massive teddy bear head*) Isn't the lovely? Apparently it's very hot inside— you shouldn't stay in for more than twenty minutes.

Theresa (*suddenly delighted*) A friend of mine used to work wearing those costumes.

Jackie Really? Did he enjoy it?

Theresa I wouldn't like to say. The last day he did was on a pier, funnily enough—dressed as a large blue duck. (*She starts to giggle*) It's quite a funny story ... he went on some Waltzers, so the children could watch Mr Duck going round and round. But the ride went too fast for him and the force caused the costume to rip. Eventually, it completely came undone, the head ripped right off, and it flew across the pier and knocked a little girl over! (*She bursts out laughing*) She was quite hysterical. Then the ride stopped, and he threw up all over his webbed feet! It was hilarious!

Sharon and Jackie have remained stone-faced throughout

Sharon Sounds a bit dangerous...

Jackie Well, it was just an idea... Who's going to show me round the pier, then?

Theresa One guided tour coming up.

Betty enters

That was quick, Nan. Finished "thinging" the "things", have you?

Betty I've left her to it. (*She sees the bear*) What's this, then? Someone shoot a stray dog?

Jackie It's a teddy bear costume.

Betty Oh. Very handy. Who's going to wear it?

Jackie (*moving to the exit*) Still waiting for a volunteer.

Theresa See you in a minute, Nan.

Sharon I'll come along. You all right on your own, Betty?

Betty Oh, yes, dear.

Theresa, Jackie and Sharon leave

Betty examines the teddy bear costume. She picks up the head and looks at it, face to face

Black-out. Music

SCENE 3

Spotlight on a sign reading "Later That Day"

The Lights come up on Sharon at the very first stages of painting the office with Jackie. They are surrounded by stacks of pastel-coloured paint pots

The music fades out

Sharon I think I'm getting high on the paint fumes already.
Jackie Shall I open a window?
Sharon Don't you dare! It's the only way I know of hallucinating and re-coating a wall at the same time!
Jackie I'm glad I picked out these colours. If you use just plain shades, it looks so dull, doesn't it?
Sharon I suppose so. Not too hot on colours myself. All our walls are covered in "flock"—it's like living in a take-away. Still, if something comes of this wild idea, we'll be able to get a place of our own. Just need a bit of money for a deposit. The pier could be our ticket.

They paint

Oh, by the way—I mentioned to Stevey about dressing up as the teddy and he said he'd give it a go.
Jackie Oh, that's terrific.
Sharon Yeah.
Jackie When will he be joining us?
Sharon Not for a few days yet. He's not allowed to leave town until cleared of all the charges.
Jackie Can't wait to meet him, he sounds—quite a character...

There is a sound of a car arriving and a door slamming

Hallo, who's this?

Sharon goes over to the door, dribbling paint on the table with the brush in her hand as she does so. She looks out

Sharon It's the ex-wife.
Jackie How does she look?
Sharon (*to Jackie*) I'm sure she's cheered up a bit since this morning. (*She looks out*) Oh, I don't know, though!

Pam enters with the receipts given by Jackie. She looks very unhappy

Pam Stop! Don't use any more of that paint. It's all going back.
Jackie What do you mean?
Pam What do I mean, Jackie? What do I mean!? I'll tell you what I mean—which paint would that be that you're using, by the way? That particular one, is it "White with a hint of sunflower" or "Turquoise with a hint of meringue"?
Sharon Is there a problem?
Pam A problem? Yes, yes, I think I'd say there is—turquoise with a hint of meringue has an air of problem about it!
Jackie I don't——
Pam All you had to do was buy some paint. Some ordinary paint. White and blue. (*To Sharon*) And she comes back with these—ludicrous—and very expensive—pastel shades! How on earth are we going to turn a profit on this place with these kind of silly extravagances? I mean, what other colours can we look forward to in the other pots? (*She examines one of the pots*) "Rose with a hint of smoked salmon"! (*She throws it down in disbelief*) Oh, well, how about "Green with a hint of gooseberry yoghurt"? Or "Brown with a hint of pork pie"!? She's turning the colour scheme into a dinner party!
Sharon I'm sure Jackie just wanted things to look nice.
Pam Nice!? Have you seen what Jackie considers nice? Look at her make-up for starters. I've never seen so many different shades of blusher on someone's face—it's like she was standing too close when an Avon Lady exploded!
Jackie I am here, you know, Pam. You can talk directly to me.
Pam (*turning to Jackie*) Have you seen the cost of all this paint? I've been scrimping and saving on all my purchasing responsibilities, drawing up careful budgets, and then you go out and buy the most expensive, most delicate, most silly paint available. It's ridiculous. Some sort of special offer, was it? Two for the price of seven!
Jackie This conversation isn't really about paint, is it?
Pam Yes, it is—it's not a personal thing.
Jackie I bought what I thought would be best. We're supposed to be doing this pier up, making it look nice. So I bought the paint accordingly.

Pam These are office walls—for people to lean on, to stick posters on—it's not necessary for them to be a tribute to Laura Ashley. I'm sorry, but I can't let you purchase any more paint.

Jackie Fine. I won't bother again.

Pam I have no idea how Michael put up with you for all those years.

Jackie At least he was happy and healthy.

Pam Healthy!? Oh, yes! I noticed how well he looked at his funeral!

Jackie Oh, this is a wonderful start, isn't it?

Pam That's not my fault, you're the one that——

Jackie I have made such an effort to try and be as——

Pam Oh, here we go, the great——

Jackie I've been sensitive to your feelings——

Pam (*shouting*) You have not! You have not!

Jackie (*shouting*) Yes, I have! I've——

Pam (*shouting*) Don't you raise your voice to me——

Jackie (*shouting*) You don't give me any alternative——

Pam (*shouting*) The suffering I've been through——

Jackie (*shouting*) Year after year of childish——

Pam (*shouting*) You have no idea! The years of——

This continues, ad-lib, at fever pitch for a few more seconds

Then as it crescendos, the teddy bear bursts into the room. It is clearly being worn by someone far too small for it and the fur is layered in huge folds, with the bottom of the legs dragging on the floor and the arms hanging down

The bear staggers grotesquely around the room. Pam screams in surprise. The teddy continues to stagger around, knocking things to the floor as it goes

What on earth!?

Jackie Who's in there?

Pam Oh, my God! Quick! It's about to faint!

Jackie Sit down!

They sit teddy down

Pam (*peering into the head*) Are you all right?

Jackie Hallo!

Pam Can you breathe!?

Jackie Get the head off!

Pam (*shouting*) Stupid fool!

Jackie (*shouting back*) I'm only trying to help!

Pam (*shouting a lot*) I'm not talking to you, I'm talking to teddy!
Sharon (*shouting*) Can we stop shouting and get the head off, please!

They proceed to unzip and unbuckle the costume. The teddy head is removed. It is Betty. Her face and hair are drenched with sweat. She gasps for air

Pam Betty! My God, woman—you could have died! What a thing to do at your age!
Jackie Are you all right?
Betty Water ... water...

Sharon grabs a cup of water and throws it into Betty's face. They all look at her in astonishment

To drink, dear, to drink.
Sharon Sorry.
Jackie Just relax now. Take it easy. (*She wipes Betty's face with a tissue*)

Sharon brings over a glass of water, which Betty gulps down

Pam What on earth were you up to?
Betty I was trying it out.
Pam Why!?
Betty To see if the children would like it.
Sharon And did they?
Betty No, they didn't! One smiled, four cried, and three were dragged away screaming.
Pam Look at the state of you. You could have had a heart attack!

Betty drinks the rest of the water

Betty Where's me tobacco?
Pam Oh, don't be ridiculous.
Betty Where is it?
Pam I said "No" and I meant it! And it's time you gave up. It's time you listened to your doctors and took care of yourself. You're not twenty-one anymore!
Betty No, and you're not forty-nine any more! You don't have to take your anger out on me!
Pam I'm not. It's just time you were told! Where are your tablets?
Betty In my bag. But I don't need them, I'm all right. I've just spent half an hour in a furry sauna, that's all.
Sharon Do you want another drink, Betty?

Betty Yes, dear.

Pam and Jackie sit by Betty checking she is OK as Sharon fetches more water

Theresa enters, with a clipboard

Theresa Oh—taking it easy again?

Harsh looks all round

What are you wearing those furry trousers for, Nan? Is it cold in here?
Betty It's a scientific experiment.
Theresa (*looking at her clipboard*) I've been talking to a cleaning company about our problem with the seagulls.
Sharon Seagulls?
Theresa Yes. Their do-dos. It seems that the Arcade roof is in fact painted green and not speckled white as we had thought. It's going to be quite expensive to get it scrubbed clean.
Pam Then it will have to wait. The budget's already gone out of control, thanks to certain people.
Jackie If you'll excuse me, I'm not staying where I'm not wanted.

Jackie walks out of the office

Theresa Is something wrong?
Sharon I better go with her, make sure she's OK.

Sharon follows Jackie out

Theresa Mum? What is this?
Pam Nothing. I had a bit of a row with Jackie, that's all.
Theresa About what?
Pam It doesn't matter. Paint. Lots of things.
Theresa It's her first day! I thought you were going to make an effort.
Pam I made no promises.
Theresa This is ridiculous. I knew it, you know. I just knew it.
Pam Don't start on me, Theresa, I'm not in the mood.
Theresa You could ruin everything. You know that, don't you?
Pam It wasn't my fault.
Theresa No, of course not—nothing ever is! You had no intention of—even giving this a chance. It doesn't matter what you destroy, so long as you have your say! Isn't that right?
Pam I said, stop it!

Theresa You're so selfish. You don't care about my feelings at all. You don't give a damn about anyone except yourself!

Pam Theresa! How dare you say that to me!

Theresa You know how important this is to all of us. Why are you here? Why don't you just stay at home and let us get on with it. If we make any money, you know I'll make sure you get your share.

Pam Your father specified my name in this will. He asked me to deal with this pier.

Theresa He asked it of all of us. As a team. We need to do this as a team. And if you won't work as part of a team, then you have to go home. Let's be honest, Mum, you don't really feel any duty to Dad. And you certainly don't have a great affection for piers. I don't understand why you came along in the first place.

Pam I'm sorry about this, Nan, it must be very embarrassing for you.

Betty Don't mind me, dear—I'm just happy to be alive.

Theresa Mum, we need to sort this out.

Pam Listen, darling; there's a lot of pressure on me right now. I've lost your father twice. Once to her. And then to God. And you expect me just to... I can't forgive her, I can't. And things are always going to happen that——

Theresa Then you should——

Pam Just let me finish... I know I've been silly, I know that. She just makes me so angry, everything about her. But that doesn't mean I don't have a right to be here. This is all I have. You, and Betty. And this pier is all I have to remember your father by. So let me do what... Just let me contribute as I can. And I will try. All right? From here on, I'll try... Now please give me a hug because you break my heart when you talk to me like that.

Theresa gives Pam a hug

Sharon enters

Sharon She's gone off for a walk. (*She picks up the teddy costume*) Come on, Betty, let's get this put away.

Pam It's all right, I'll do it. (*She stuffs the costume back into the box*) Betty, I think perhaps you should go home. You look a bit peaky.

Betty All right, Pam.

Pam Shall I leave the box here?

Theresa Yes, I'll put it away later.

Pam (*to Betty*) Come on, then.

Pam exits with Betty

Theresa Dad must have known this would happen; Mum and Jackie using each other like punchbags. I have a horrible feeling that it was part of his idea.

Sharon He did have a bizarre sense of humour.

Theresa Yes. Well, I say "Yes"—I hear that he did. We didn't really see much of it at home. There's not many opportunities for being light-hearted after twenty years with my mother.

Sharon Well, let me tell you—at work, he was a riot. So funny. He had me in stitches. At the Christmas party, I laughed so hard, I fell off my chair—literally, I really did.

Theresa Must have been a very funny joke to make you do that.

Sharon It was... Though the bottle of Vodka helped.

Theresa It's strange, isn't it, that you knew a different Michael to the one I did. The same man, but other aspects of him. You get the same idea when you talk to Mum, or Jackie—or Nan. He was different to all of them. It's like a jigsaw puzzle. You only get a complete picture when we're all together.

Sharon Blimey, that was dense... Come on, let's get on with sorting this dump out.

Theresa Yes, you're right. No point letting ourselves get dragged down by it all. Yes—we should just get on with it, like you say. That was very forthright of you, Sharon. It's nice to see you taking the bull by the horns.

Sharon Oh, I can be decisive and full of ideas, when the mood takes me. Deep down, I'm a born leader. Right—what the hell do we do now?

Theresa Fund-raising.

Sharon Good. Yes. Actually, I have been meaning to talk to you about something.

Theresa You've had an idea?

Sharon Yes. But only if you think now's the right time to...?

Theresa Absolutely. Go on.

Sharon Well, you know I eat too much chocolate.

Theresa Yes?

Sharon When I get really guilty, I do some aerobics. Go to a class or listen to a tape, watch a video at my mate's house. And—I'm quite familiar with how it all works, all the moves, exercises, all the aerobicising—I thought I could set up a class—and charge for it.

Theresa An aerobics class—here?

Sharon Yeah. It would be the world's first aerobic pier! With me as the teacher, the instructor, you know; standing at the front with a pink leotard and clenched buttocks.

Theresa (*unconvinced*) Have you tried this before?

Sharon No, but I'm game. And it's an idea for raising some money, isn't it?

Theresa Yes, but you should practise first, don't you think? Before throwing yourself in at the deep end.

Sharon You're right... (*A thought strikes her*) I'll practise on you lot! You, Pam, Jackie and Betty. You can be my class.

Theresa I don't know if that's a very good idea.

Sharon Of course it is. Who else am I gonna get? Look. You and Jackie are game for anything—right? And I'm sure you can persuade your mum to join in. Betty as well, maybe.

Theresa Well——

Sharon Come on, support me! I'm making an effort here! Theresa, at some point one of us has to get the ball rolling—we're all gonna have to come up with things like this—it's the only way we're going to get the extra money coming in. Even if we get a lottery grant, we still have to match the money. Every penny counts—right? And I can't do it without the help of you four. So—come on—it'll be fun!

Theresa All right—if you really think it's the right thing to do.

Sharon And the others—will you persuade them for me? Will you?

Theresa Yes.

Sharon Really!?

Theresa Yes! Yes, all right!

Sharon Great! Well, no point wasting time! I'll go now and start sorting something out. First thing tomorrow morning, ten o'clock, OK? We can do it every day—give us all a healthy start, and by the end of the month we'll have a really good routine going! Make sure everyone turns up in suitable clothing.

Theresa And what is suitable clothing?

Sharon Stretch pants, leg warmers, leotard. What have you got?

Theresa (*referring to her clothes*) This, one other skirt and a green cardigan.

Sharon Fine. So long as they stretch!

Sharon leaps about with excitement and runs out of the door

Theresa looks down at her clothes

Black-out

Music: aerobics tape—heavy beat, pop music. As the music plays, the office furniture is cleared to the sides and corners of the room

SCENE 4

A sign above the stage reads "The Next Morning"

The Lights come up on a stereo system playing the aerobics music. The floor space is clear, apart from a few towels scattered about

Pam enters, wearing her usual clothes, plus a pair of old leg warmers and a headband. She is followed by Betty in an extremely ill-fitting old-fashioned tracksuit

Pam (*shouting over the music*) Hallo!? Sharon!? (*She turns the music volume down*) Where is she, then? Must have gone to the ladies.
Betty Eh?
Pam The ladies.

Theresa enters in a skirt, purple stockings, plimsolls and a green cardigan

Theresa Morning, everyone.
Pam Morning.
Betty Hallo, dear.

Theresa kisses them both

Theresa (*to Betty*) Where on earth did you get that tracksuit?
Betty It was your grandad's. He had his coronary in it.

Sharon enters, dressed as a cross between an olympic gymnast and Sid Vicious

Sharon Morning! Ready to swing your cellulite left to right? Ready for action?

They all groan

Good. (*She turns the volume of the music up high*)

The door opens and in walks Jackie. She wears a new, young and stylish multi-coloured low cut lycra exercising suit, with all matching accessories

Pam stares at her in disbelief. Jackie ignores this and starts some preparatory stretches

Shall we start, then? Good. (*She stands in front of them and presents the moves as she describes them*)

The others awkwardly follow her actions with varying degrees of hopelessness

And—stretch out first ... left arm; stretch ... right arm stretch ... feel the burn, feel the callenetic ... think Cher, think Fonda—Jane, not Henry—

and now step from side to side ... and forward and back ... good ... run on the spot ... or walk if you feel too old.

Betty and Pam start walking on the spot. However, when Pam notices Jackie is running on the spot, she does so also

All right, I want you to make turns now one by one, as I call your name out. Jackie, turn.

Jackie does a full turn

Theresa, turn.

Theresa does a full turn

Pam, turn.

Pam turns

Betty, turn.

Betty is distracted

Betty, turn.

Nothing

Betty! Betty!
Betty Eh?
Sharon Turn! Do a turn!

Betty turns immediately on the spot, adding to the move a quick soft shoe shuffle

Keep jogging now. And—relax. (*She turns off the music and stays by the machine*)

Pam grabs her towel

Pam Well, that wasn't so bad.
Sharon That was just the warm-up, Pam.

Pam's face drops

Now for the real action!

Snap Black-out

Music starts immediately: we hear the Eighties chart record Hooked on Classics, *or another piece of music if preferred. Spotlight on a sign reading "One Month Later". The Lights then cross-fade back to the office and rise on their now well-practised aerobics routine. The moves are known by heart and performed to the music. Jackie and Sharon are very slick, with Theresa working hard but lacking natural rhythm. Betty's actions are often minimal, just doing the hand gestures, or completely different to everybody else's. Pam frequently tries to keep up with Jackie, but with limited success. Pelvic thrusts, scissors and bicycling moves are all possibilities for this sequence, which should aim to be as comic as possible. On various occasions, they bump into each other or appear destined to fall flat on their faces. The routine builds to a leg-kicking finale and they all hit a dynamic final pose as the music climaxes*

Snap Black-out

Scene 5

During the Black-out, the office set is cleared. Music plays

To cover the time needed for the set change, the figure of "Stevey" crosses the stage dressed in—and obscured by—the teddy bear costume. He strolls along the front of the stage in a masculine manner, carrying sandwich boards that read, "Save Our Pier". The actress playing Jackie is the person representing the persona of "Stevey" on this occasion. Spotlight on a sign reading "Another Month Later"

Scene 6

The Lights come up on the deck of the pier. A clear, sunny day. Sea and bird noises in the background

The pleasure pier setting incorporates railings overlooking the sea, strings of coloured light bulbs, and a row of deck-chairs. A sign displays a spooky figure pointing the way to the ghost train

Betty sits on a deck-chair C, stitching together sections of an advertising banner. She wears a "Kiss me quick" hat

Sharon stands behind, wiping the dust off a box of coloured bulbs

Betty Where's your fella gone? He's only been here five minutes and he's disappeared again.

Sharon Theresa's got Stevey dressed in that teddy bear costume—the one you tried on—he's out walking the streets and meeting kids. It's funny, isn't it? Children like giant cuddly bears. They trust them. They'd get scared off if an adult approached them——

Betty Especially one with "vomit" written on his forehead.

Sharon But they don't mind saying hallo to a teddy bear. In theory, anyway. We'll see how he gets on. He's just happy to be doing something.

Betty There. Finished. (*She shows that she has finished re-stitching the banner*)

Sharon Let me give you a hand. (*She takes the banner from Betty and they stretch it out*)

It says "Welcome to the Pleasure Pier", but Betty has stitched the two halves together with one half of the lettering upside down

Betty (*not realizing*) Made a good job of that.

Sharon Yes...

Betty Help me roll it up.

They do so

Another job done! What shall I do with myself now?

Sharon Why don't you just take it easy for a bit. Put your feet up. Do you want a drink or something?

Betty No, dear, thank you. Look, why don't you come and join me. Come on. Come and sit down. Take the weight off your hair.

Sharon joins Betty, sitting on one of the other deck-chairs

You should get some rest, what with all your aerobicising. How's your class going?

Sharon Very good. Got twenty regulars now—made nearly three hundred pound.

Betty Well done.

Sharon Won't go very far, of course. But every bit helps, eh?

Betty Yes, dear, that's right.

They look out to sea. We hear a seagull fly past

I like it here. You get the pebble beach and all the chalets.

Sharon Well, a few of them. Not many left now, really, is there?

Betty No. They all got washed away. Shame, really.

Sharon Did you ever have a chalet here?

Betty Oh, yes. (*She points*) See where that blue hotel is?

Sharon God, you've got good eyes.

Betty Carrots, dear.

Sharon The tall one?

Betty Yes. It was just in front of that.

Sharon Really? Nothing much at all there now.

Betty It all crumbled into the sea.

Sharon We could have done with it now—extra office space!

Betty Not likely. There was hardly room enough to swing a cat... Not that we had a cat. We had a rabbit. Nice little place, though. Couple of chairs, table for the flask, a shelf for your flip-flops... And on the wall, we had a painting of a clown with tears rolling down his cheeks. Weather was always miserable.

Sharon Maybe that's why he was crying.

Betty But it's all gone now.

The teddy bear enters, moving with the characteristics of Stevey. It is actually the actress playing Jackie inside the costume

Teddy taps Betty on the shoulder and she turns with a yelp of surprise

Oh, my gawd!

Sharon It's all right, it's only Stevey.

Teddy gives Sharon a hug

Theresa enters

Theresa He's been very popular with the children in the High Street—most of them anyway. And I think the rest will be all right once they've calmed down. (*She peers into the teddy bear's mouth*) Stevey—look, I know you must be tired out, but someone really needs to have a look at that candyfloss machine. Any chance of seeing what you can do?

Stevey the teddy bear salutes

Sharon My god! We seem to have caught him in one of his more efficient moods! Come on, Teddy, I'll join you—Operation Candyfloss, here we go!

Sharon and teddy head up the pier, cuddling each other

Theresa They still seem to be in love, don't they?

Betty Seem to be.

Theresa Well, even if they're not, at least they're having plenty of … you know what. They've been at it every five minutes since Stevey got here. Still, good luck to them—at least someone is having—having a little bit of the other round here. They're probably wandering down the pier to have some more now! I hope they're … you know… "Safe".

Betty Oh yes, the planks are nailed down good and solid.

Theresa sits in the deck-chair next to Betty

Theresa Look, now that they're out of the way. I've got something to tell you… We've had a fax—from [CELEBRITY]'s agent. I know this sounds ridiculous, but, apparently, she's actually interested in doing the concert for us. Nothing definite yet, mind. It may come to nothing at all—but, well, it's a real possibility. Can you believe it!?

Betty Oh, Theresa!

Theresa Not a word to anyone yet, though, I don't want to raise their hopes. But—I just had to tell someone, I couldn't keep it all to myself. We'll get a decision soon, once the agent has had a chat to her. Could be any minute—exciting, isn't it!?

Betty Exciting? It's a blooming miracle!

Theresa But it's not definite, by any means—you must keep it a secret. Don't tell anyone at all. Not a word to anybody.

Betty I understand, dear.

Sharon comes back in

Sharon Stevey needs some oil, have we got any?

Betty Never mind that, we've got [CELEBRITY] coming here.

Sharon Have we?

Theresa Nan! No, no, absolutely not. We haven't.

Betty We might have!

Theresa Only might. Maybe. I wasn't going to say anything until it was more certain.

Sharon I knew she would come here if you asked her. I had a feeling in my water.

Theresa Might come here. Might. Might!

Betty We'll have to get the place cleaned up.

Theresa Let's just not think about it. Just forget about it for now. OK? Please. I shouldn't have even said anything. Now what was it you wanted?

Sharon bursts out singing, giving us a few lines from the most famous song of our celebrity

Don't do this.

Betty sings a line herself, in similar vein, but getting the words comically wrong

I knew I shouldn't have told you! Why do I do these things? Sharon, snap out of it!

Sharon does

The oil. You'll find it on the shelf in the back room of the arcade.
Sharon That's where we were, but didn't see any—what does it look like?
Theresa It's in an oil can with "Oil" written on it in very big letters.
Sharon Oh, no wonder I missed it!

Sharon exits, singing as she goes

Theresa Honestly, Nan! I won't make that mistake again in a hurry. Let's just keep it between the three of us now.
Betty All right, dear.

Pam enters from the office side of the pier

Pam What's all this about [CELEBRITY]?
Theresa (*to Betty*) Are you telepathic?
Pam Theresa? Tell me.
Theresa How did you know?
Pam There's a fax from her agent on your desk. Have they rung back yet?
Theresa No, I'm still waiting.
Pam It's just what we need, you know. It could bring in about fifty thousand pounds. Plus it's great for publicity. This is just what we needed, couldn't have come at a better time.
Theresa But it might not happen.
Pam It has to happen. If they come back, changing their minds, you'll just have to ring them up and persuade them. Offer her some expenses and a hot lunch. That'll bring her round.

Betty gets out of the deck-chair

Check the fax machine while you're in there, Nan.
Betty In the toilet?
Pam Oh, I thought you were going in the office. In that case, pop in when you're done and have a look.

Betty Right.

Betty exits

Pam How's everything else going?
Theresa Not too bad. Stevey's having a crack at the candyfloss machine.
Pam I trust he's taken the costume off, before he starts squirting oil everywhere.
Theresa I'm sure he has. (*Suddenly worried*) I better just check.

Theresa is about to exit in the direction of Sharon and Stevey, when we hear an explosion. Theresa and Pam gasp in surprise

Theresa runs off, in the direction of the noise

Pam (*shouting after her*) What's happened!? Are they all right? Oh, my! Are you OK?
Theresa (*off*) She's fine, she's fine. Do you want to get a damp cloth or something?

Theresa enters with Sharon, her hair thick with candyfloss, plus small amounts scattered on her face and clothes

Sharon At least it's not bunged up any more.
Pam What happened?
Sharon I don't know really. One minute he was oiling it and the next there was this sort of rush of pink. Is my hair in a mess?
Pam No worse than usual!
Theresa Let me get you a cloth.
Sharon Don't worry, I may as well let it dry, then I can just brush it out.
Theresa Are you sure?
Sharon Yeah. Besides, I might get peckish. (*She yells off*) Stevey—leave it! It might explode again!
Theresa (*to Sharon*) How does he see the electrics, wearing a teddy bear head?
Sharon It's a special gift.
Pam Come on, you can't stand around like that, you'll start attracting flies.

Pam and Sharon exit together after a moment

Betty enters from the other direction and beckons Theresa over

Betty Pssst! Pssst!

Theresa What is it?

Betty It's me, dear. We've received another fax.

Theresa We have? Did you bring it?

Betty Yes, dear. (*She carries on the whole fax machine with the faxed letter hanging out of it*) Here it is.

Theresa tears the paper from the machine and reads it. She becomes excited

Theresa She's agreed! I don't believe it! We've done it! [CELEBRITY] is going to do a concert for us! We did it! We did it!

Betty and Theresa share a joyful hug. Theresa then reads on. Her face registers some concern

Betty What else does it say? Everything all right?

Theresa Erm ... well, there are some conditions ... it's not completely plain sailing, but—no, I think it will be fine, I really do. I think we've got her! (*She puts the paper away in a pocket*) Oh, Nan, I'm so excited! Oh! (*She clutches her heart*) Oh dear—I think I'm in shock. We need some support acts—I'll have to get on the phone. And the theatre needs to be brought up to scratch. We better talk to Stevey. I wonder if she has a caravan.

Betty I don't think she's even got a chalet.

Theresa No, these big stars have caravans. To do their make-up in and sign autographs.

Betty What if she arrives by helicopter? Where's she gonna land?

Theresa We'll have to tell the local papers—and the television! Oh, I'm having trouble breathing...! Oh, Nan, what a day! (*She takes the fax machine*) We better get this plugged back in. ITN might be trying to get through!

Betty and Theresa exit, full of excitement

Music. Black-out

SCENE 7

Theresa, Pam, Betty and Sharon on the pier deck, as before

Huge commotion. Sharon is wearing a rubber ring with a swan head on it and flippers, plus a red nose. Theresa has two Punch and Judy puppets, one on each hand. Betty carries a clipboard. Pam is struggling to assemble a deck chair. They are all talking at once when the Lights come up

Theresa Then we should decide between us——
Betty Whose go is it, then? I can't keep up.
Sharon It'll work for the kids——
Betty Let's do it again from the top.
Sharon But I don't know about the adults——
Theresa There may not be many kids——
Betty Yes, there will be.
Theresa Will there?
Betty Cheaper than babysitters.
Sharon You see, that's right.

The discussion continues, all speaking at once, until Pam's voice is heard above everyone else's

Pam Will somebody please help me with this bloody deck-chair!!

Silence. Theresa sorts the deck-chair out in a matter of seconds. She then squats behind it, her hand puppets peering over the edge

Theresa (*in the voice of Mr Punch*) That's the way to do it!
Pam She doesn't get it from me…

Pam sits in the deck chair as Theresa emerges from behind it

　　Now, where were we?
Sharon Should we have an act for children in the show or not?
Pam It's an afternoon show, there are bound to be children there. But that doesn't mean we have to entertain them.
Theresa I think whatever we do has to basically appeal to adults.
Pam Yes.
Betty Definitely.
Pam So that's you off the list, Sharon.
Sharon Right… Maybe I could do aerobics instead—as a warm-up for the audience.

They all stare at her

　　Bad idea. (*She removes her red nose*)
Betty What about the puppets?
Theresa I'm not good enough. Cross me out.
Pam So what does that leave us with?
Betty Just the dance school, the magician—and [CELEBRITY].
Pam (*proudly*) Oh, yes…

Betty Will she be wanting lunch?

Theresa Yes, we'll need some catering.

Sharon I could do that—I'll make a big vat of chilli.

Theresa She might be vegetarian.

Sharon I could put some carrots in it.

Pam Look, all that sort of thing can wait. The point is, do we have a show that's long enough?

Sharon What about a raffle?

Betty Or some bingo. They could have numbers in their programmes.

Sharon Yes!

Theresa Great idea, Nan. And I'm sure the dance school will do some extra bits if we ask.

Sharon That's right. We were making it too complicated. Get all the acts we've already got to stretch a bit, add some speeches, raffle and bingo— and we're there! They'll sit through anything because they'll know our big star is coming up.

Pam Good. We're all agreed then? What a waste of energy that turned out to be. Let's get to the theatre and get on with all the technical necessaries. Who's coming?

Betty I better had, I've got the clipboard.

Pam leads the way off stage, with Betty following

After a moment, Jackie edges carefully into view

Jackie Hallo.

Theresa Hi, Jackie.

Jackie Have they gone?

Theresa Yes. Is there a problem?

Jackie comes on, carrying a funeral urn. She places it at the front of the stage. Sharon and Theresa stare at the urn, silent

Jackie I didn't think it fair to Pam and Betty, but I thought you'd be all right about it. I hope you don't mind me bringing it along. It's your father. It's Michael's ashes. I sort of felt he should be here. In whatever form. I'll leave him there for now, so he can have this moment with us.

Sharon You feeling all right, Jackie? Can we get you a strait-jacket or anything?

Jackie I know, it is a bit mad of me. But—our relationship was very spiritual and—I feel he's still around... It just felt wrong having his ashes just sitting there at home. I thought they should be part of all this. That Michael should be represented here.

Sharon Well, he'll certainly be entertained! It's—just a bit morbid, though—isn't it?
Jackie I don't think so. It's nice to have something. I talk to him occasionally.
Sharon In the urn?
Jackie Yes. You probably think I'm crazy.
Sharon It had crossed my mind…!
Jackie You don't object, do you, Theresa?
Theresa No … no. I think it's—nice.
Sharon Perhaps I should leave you three to chat?

Pause

Yes … yes, perhaps I should…

Jackie and Theresa continue to stare at the urn

They must be needing some help … at the … at the … what's-it… (*She edges off*) See you all later…

Sharon exits

Theresa It's odd, isn't it? To think that's all there is left.

Jackie puts her arm around Theresa

Jackie Do you think he'd be proud of us? Of the work we're doing to his pier?
Theresa Yes. And a bit surprised. I bet he never thought you and Mum would get along.
Jackie We hardly do that, Theresa. She hasn't spoken a word to me in four weeks and looks at me like I'm the scum of the earth.
Theresa I know, but it's a step forward, isn't it?

The Lights slowly fade to Black-out as they stand together, staring at the urn

CURTAIN

ACT II

A sign above the stage reads "Three Months Later"

The Lights rise on the 50s theatre at the end of the pier. The backdrop is a shimmering golden curtain

Jackie enters, carrying a microphone on a stand, and places it C

Jackie (*calling into the wings*) Is this where you want it?

Theresa enters

Theresa Just make sure it's right in the middle, then we'll get a giant spotlight to centre on it.

Pam enters, hassled, clipboard in hand

Pam We're never going to be ready.
Theresa It'll be fine.
Pam Will it?
Theresa Mum, have a little bit of trust for a change. Things don't always turn out for the worst, you know.
Pam I'll remember that the next time I get married.
Jackie Something wrong?
Pam Nothing that needs concern you, Jackie.
Jackie Sorry I asked! Did you get through to [CELEBRITY]'s agent?
Theresa There's no answer. But everything's fine, I'm sure. I bet she can't wait to get here. She's a big fan of piers, apparently.
Jackie I think we all are by now. I hope she'll come early and have a wander round. It's like reliving your childhood, walking along the planks—seeing the rigging and the sea underneath. I still get moments of panic that I'm going to fall through one of the gaps...!
Pam (*aside*) Not very likely with those hips! This microphone stand is in the wrong place—it should be in the middle.
Jackie It is in the middle.

Pam No, it isn't. Not in the middle at all. Honestly, if you want anything done you have to do it yourself.

Jackie The stand is in the middle!

Pam No, it isn't! (*She moves the stand about four inches to the left*) That's the middle!

Theresa Please! We don't have time for this!

Black-out

(*To the back of the auditorium*) Ah, Stevey! Is that you up there? Stevey?

A spotlight comes on C. *They all edge into it*

That's the light for our star then, is it? Stevey?

Pam He can't hear you.

Theresa (*shouting and gesturing*) Is that the light for our star? Um—if it is, could you move it a few inches to the left—so the microphone stand is exactly in the middle of it? And could you perhaps add a bit of colour? (*She waits, but nothing happens*) I'll presume that's a "no" then, shall I? (*She squints and looks out again*) What's he wearing?

Jackie Oh, erm—it's a furry seal.

Theresa Any particular reason? A union thing, is it?

Jackie They were using a chap in a seal costume to promote the Sealife Centre down the promenade and Stevey felt it was unfair competition.

Pam So he nicked it?

Jackie I think he prefers to think of it as setting the animal free from captivity. It's made out of poly-cotton so I don't quite see the logic, but it seems to make him happy.

There is a loud screech from the stage speakers

Theresa I think he's found the sound.

Pam Either that or he just clubbed the seal to death.

Theresa Can we hear the sound, Stevey? (*She gestures*) The sound?

Nothing happens

This is silly, he can't hear me.

Suddenly we hear the music of the backing track blasting through the speakers. Theresa gives an enthusiastic thumbs up and they dance a little to the music. After a few moments, it stops and the Lights return to normal

Well, I suppose that's the technical rehearsal over with. Went very well,

I think. We ought to make sure the costume gets back to them, we don't want any bad feeling.

Pam I'll have a word with him.

Theresa If you wouldn't mind. And make sure he's wearing proper clothes when he meets Miss [CELEBRITY].

Pam It will be a pleasure.

Jackie Makes you pause, doesn't it?

Theresa Hm?

Jackie When you think about it. [CELEBRITY] coming here. Actually standing right here.

Theresa Yes.

Pam touches the microphone stand

Jackie It's like a dream, isn't it? Something extraordinary. Beautiful and romantic.

Betty enters, carrying a clipboard in one hand and a pot of seafood in the other. She wears a black sweatshirt with the word "Crew" written on it. A bunch of keys hangs from her belt

Betty Anyone fancy a whelk?

Pam A what?

Betty A whelk. A whelk. I got them on the promenade this morning, kept them in the fridge.

Theresa What fridge?

Betty The star's fridge.

Jackie You've been keeping whelks in [CELEBRITY]'s fridge?

Betty Yes! I'm sure she won't mind.

Pam It'll stink of vinegar. She'll open the fridge door to put in her Lucozade and her caviar and she'll get a whiff of Sarson's right up her nostrils. What on earth were you thinking of?

Betty Don't be daft. Have one.

Pam No, thank you. I don't like the look of them.

Betty I think they're gorgeous-looking. They remind me of my dad's old earplugs.

Pam Oh, super—gets more charming by the second.

Betty Here—hold these for a second, I've got work to do.

Pam reluctantly takes the seafood pot from Betty and stares at the whelks with revulsion

Theresa Yes, back to business. What's the news?

Betty wipes her hands clean on her trousers

Betty I've done the final schedule for tonight; for the artistes.

Theresa Good. So what's the running order?

Betty (*checking her clipboard*) You get the comic first, followed by the presentation from the dance school and then the magician with his glamorous assistant. Though she can't be that glamorous 'cos they're arriving in a Reliant Robin. Then you get the speech by the Mayor, followed by our own little contribution, then our big star for the finale.

Jackie Sounds fantastic.

Theresa Doesn't it? Are all the dressing-rooms ready?

Betty In the area of having a chair, yes. In the area of having a toilet roll, no.

Theresa Can we do that, then?

Betty Not my department.

Pam I'll do it. Where are they?

Jackie I don't think we have any. I think we used them all up in the foyer.

Pam Something else for the shopping list!

Jackie I'll pop out and get some.

Pam If you're sure?

Jackie Yes, I'm pretty certain I can manage that.

Pam Just plain white, though, Jackie. Don't be tempted by the double-quilted pastel bog roll, will you?

Theresa Stop it, Mum.

Jackie It's all right, Theresa. At least she talks to me these days.

Pam Only because I have to.

Theresa Have you finished, Mother? We have [CELEBRITY] coming here, for Heaven's sake! Can we not squabble over do-do paper!? (*She turns to Jackie*) Get some white—and some of the more expensive.

Pam Why?

Theresa International singing stars are used to a bit of luxury, we can't supply her with rolls of cheap sandpaper like you used to leave us with at home.

Pam It's all right if you crunch it up a bit first.

Theresa No!

Pam Every penny counts.

Theresa Not after tonight. After tonight, everything will be fine. So let's allow ourself the odd seventeen pence of wild extravagance.

Jackie Look, let's just compromise; I'll go to Safeway. It'll be better quality, but at a sensible price.

Theresa Perfect.

Betty So that's sorted, then, is it? Another earth-shattering executive decision under our belts? Because we have got a few other things on our plate, you know.

Theresa It's all right, we're on schedule. No need to panic. What's next? Anything else Jackie needs to buy?

We hear the ringing of a mobile phone. All look around

Phone. Where's the mobile phone? Who's got it?
Jackie Pam—you had it last night.
Pam No, I did not. When did I have it last night?
Theresa It doesn't matter who had it last night—where is it now?

The phone continues to ring

Betty Oh, hang on, hold your horses. (*She discovers the mobile phone, stuffed up her sweatshirt*)
Theresa How on earth did it wind up in there?
Betty Bugger only knows. I'm off to the dressing-room. (*She passes the mobile phone to Pam*)

Betty exits

Pam (*answering the phone*) Hallo? ... Yes, it is. ... Who? ... (*Suddenly excited*) Oh, yes, hallo! ... We're just getting things ready for her. ... Yes! ... (*Suddenly serious*) What!? ... What!? ... Oh, my God!
Theresa What's happened?
Pam (*into the phone*) But how can this happen!? ... No, we didn't! ... What!? ... Oh. ... Well, yes, I'm sure you are—but what are we supposed to do? ... Is there absolutely—I mean—is there another day when she... But, I mean; I'm just... I'm speechless...
Theresa Mum? Mum? (*She yells*) Mum!! What's happened?
Pam (*into the phone*) Yes. ... Goodbye... (*She turns the phone off*) It's off. [CELEBRITY] had to cancel.
Theresa What!?
Jackie No!
Pam She has the flu.
Theresa She can't sing?
Pam She can't speak!
Jackie I don't believe this.
Pam You'd think there was a drug or something she could take. What did they give Judy Garland?
Jackie Are they sending someone else?
Pam No, they're not! And she hasn't got another free date for six months! We should sue them.
Theresa We can't. They made the clauses clear at the beginning to cover

things like this. In the event of illness, they simply cancel and that's that.
We weren't paying her—so, I mean, what can we do?

Jackie But we're sold out!

Betty walks back on to the stage

I can't believe she can't come! Why didn't they tell us yesterday?

Pam She thought she'd be better! What is she playing at!

Betty Am I crossing someone off the schedule?

Pam We'll have to cancel the show.

Theresa We can't, we can't.

Betty Who am I crossing off?

Pam [CELEBRITY], Nan; she's not coming. She's not coming!

Betty (*after a pause*) Well, that's a bit of a bugger, isn't it?

Jackie People will want their money back.

Pam The whole affair is down the toilet! We've spent thousands on this
already—we can't afford to put this show on again. And if we end up
cancelling, the whole pier is finished. It's over! It's over!

Theresa Calm down, Mum!

Pam Given the circumstances, this is as calm as you get!

Betty What do we do?

Jackie Can we get someone to take her place—at short notice?

Pam (*sarcastically*) Oh, wonderful idea—I'll ring Barbra Streisand. She's
probably out on the mud cockling, but I'll ask her to pop in on her way back!

Jackie It was just a suggestion.

Betty We can still do the rest of the show.

Theresa Yes—people will still have a good time.

Pam With that line-up! We were signalling the death of Variety as it was!
People are coming to see [CELEBRITY], that's the reason they're all turning
out. She's why we're doing the show in the first place. There's no way out
of this. She's up to her eyeballs in Night Nurse and we've had it! For good!

All are silenced for a moment

Betty Unless we just pretend.

Pam What!?

Betty Get someone to pretend to be her. People in these parts wouldn't know
the real [CELEBRITY] if she slapped them round the face with a wet fish. Get
someone to dress up as her and go on in her place—they won't know the
difference.

Pam Of course they will!

Betty It's all pensioners coming—most of them have got National Health
glasses and can't see a thing at any rate. Give them a couple of pints of cider,

just to make sure, and they'll have so much trouble focusing, they won't notice a thing.

Pam Honestly, Mum—you do come out with some strange ideas.

Betty Have you got a better one?

Pam Not at the moment, no.

Jackie I think Betty's right. Get a look-alike.

Pam What!?

Jackie No-one will notice if it's done well, and everyone'll be happy.

Pam Oh! Don't be silly, it will never work.

Theresa It might…

Pam Theresa!

Theresa It might! For God's sake, we have to think of something!

Pam Don't you shout at me!

Theresa What else do you expect me to do!?

Pam Just stop it!!

A momentary silence

Sharon enters smiling, oblivious to the situation. She is singing the opening bars of a famous song by our celebrity

After a moment, she realises everyone is staring at her with a look that could kill

Sharon Did I come at a bad moment?

Theresa [CELEBRITY] can't make it. She's cancelled.

Sharon Oh Jesus!

Theresa She's got the flu.

Sharon What are we gonna do?

Pam Three options so far, Sharon; Theresa wants us to carry on with the worst ever show on God's earth and no star; Jackie has suggested we go in search of Streisand on the off-chance she pulled over at the seafront this morning for a saveloy and chips; and Betty votes that we keep it all under our hats and bring in a fake! Which of these brilliant ideas would you go for?

Sharon Well, in the circumstances… I think we should bring in a fake.

Pam I don't believe this!

Sharon You know—one of those lookey-likeys.

Theresa That's right—there are agencies that specialise in them. All we have to do is——

Pam You can't do that. They only *impersonate* the stars, you'll never ever get them to say they're the real thing. They'll never agree to that. We would have to admit it's a fake, and that would defeat the whole point; everyone would ask for their money back.

Sharon Yeah—actually, Pam's right. She is right.

Theresa Then we'll have to think of something else. All this time and money is not going to waste… So… If we can't get a professional look-alike … then someone else will just have to dress up as [CELEBRITY], pretend to be the real thing, and hope nobody notices.

Pam Well, that settles it; I'm going to kill myself.

Theresa Just wait a second, Mum—listen; all they would have to do is sing a few notes, or even just say a few words. We'll say she has a cold and can't manage any more than that, but will be happy to sign autographs backstage. And she could just do the raffle or something.

Pam Without a voice?

Theresa Just picking the ticket out of the bucket.

Pam And you think seven hundred theatre-goers would accept [CELEBRITY]'s hand in a bucket as worth twenty-five quid?

Theresa They'll have seen her, won't they? They'll go home and say they saw her—in the flesh, in the theatre——

Pam In a bucket.

Theresa If they thought she'd made the effort to come all this way, that would be enough. As long as she sings a bit; just one chorus or something. Don't look at me like that! It's worth a go, isn't it? What have we got to lose?

Pam Apart from spending twenty years in jail? Nothing, I suppose.

Betty Who's going to do it?

Pam Nobody's going to do anything—it's ridiculous.

Sharon Can anyone sing?

Jackie One of us!?

Sharon It'll have to be.

Pam This is madness!

Theresa We need someone of the right age … someone who can sing… Mum?

Pam What?

Theresa You used to sing.

Pam In the bath, I did! Not at the London Palladium! Don't you look at me— I'm not doing it—no way!

Theresa You have to.

Pam I don't have to do anything!

Theresa Do it for me, for the pier.

Pam I said no! Me as [CELEBRITY]? If she found out, she'd crucify me!

Betty But we'll make sure she doesn't find out.

Theresa It has to be you. Come on—do it for Dad.

Pam Don't bring your father into this, I'm not giving into emotional blackmail.

Theresa We don't have a choice. Look, there isn't time to argue. The show is in four hours. And you are going on as [CELEBRITY] and that's that. And if you don't—I'll never speak to you again!

Pam Theresa!

Theresa I mean it! Don't let me down again. I need you to do this. Please. Please!

Pam Theresa, it's not that I don't want to—it's that I can't!

Theresa But you can! I saw you at the Club that night with Dad. (*To the others*) They had a "Stars in Your Eyes" competition and Mum came second. She won a box of Milk Tray.

Sharon There you go! Did you do it as [CELEBRITY]?

Pam No, Nana Maskouri.

Betty Well, that's a start!

Theresa And she's a member of the amateur operatic society.

Pam That was years ago!

Theresa So?

Sharon Come on, Pam.

Pam Aren't we forgetting something? Costume! You've seen what she wears—I don't have that kind of dress.

Jackie We can hire one, that isn't a problem. And I have a cassette in the Astra, so you can practise her voice.

Pam I still can't believe we're even discussing this.

Betty You do have a decent singing voice, Pam. You always did have.

Sharon We'll all help you. You won't be out there on your own, not really.

Theresa The final decision has to be yours. And it has to be made now... Mum?

Pam All right. All right, all right. I must be insane!

They all cheer with relief. Theresa gives Pam a big kiss and a hug

Theresa Thank you, thank you.

Pam (*suddenly forthright*) Right—now listen: I want help from everyone; I want that cassette, a fabulous costume, and a bloody good wig! So get to it!

Black-out. Instrumental big band music plays us through to the next scene

SCENE 2

A sign above the stage reads "One Hour to Show Time"

The music continues as Betty crosses the stage with a reel of cable

Jackie enters with the urn of ashes

She places it at the side of the stage and blows it a kiss

As Jackie exits, Theresa and Sharon enter from opposite sides and meet in the middle. Sharon wears an apron covered in make-up smudges

Theresa How are you getting on? Is Mum ready?
Sharon I think so. She's very nervous.
Theresa One hour to go. I'd better pop in and see how she's——
Sharon No! She says she wants to be on her own for a few moments.
Theresa Does she look anything like [CELEBRITY]?
Sharon Well—I've given her a bit of a Hollywood-style make-over, you know—using the best that Superdrug had to offer. And the wig is very good—under the circumstances—and allowing for the severe damage when we ran over it. I think you'll be quite surprised though, all in all. And I think people really will believe it is actually the real [CELEBRITY]. As long as you accept that recent life has been particularly hard on her.

Betty enters, clipboard in hand and with headphones round her neck

Betty Oh, there you are.
Sharon I better tell her it's time to make an appearance.

Sharon exits

Betty I've told the other acts that our star is a very private person and they must stay in their dressing-rooms until called. They didn't like that very much. The magician and his assistant threatened to go home. But as their Reliant Robin had only just made it here in the first place, they didn't have much choice. How are you getting on, dear?
Theresa I've been going through my lines. I've not been a compere before. It's a bit daunting.
Betty You'll be fine.

Jackie enters

Jackie There are already lots of people in the foyer.
Theresa Don't mention that in front of Mum. Sharon says she's a bit nervous.

Sharon runs on stage

Sharon She's coming! She's coming! (*She spots the urn*) I'll move this— I don't think Pam's quite in the mood for it. (*She hides the urn in the front corner of the stage and pulls the curtain round to hide it*)

Jackie It's all getting very tense, isn't it?

Theresa Yes, I've already had three aspirins today. I get these heads.

Sharon (*looking off*) Look out, here she comes. Now, she's still a bit unsure of herself, so everyone give her a supportive smile.

They all fix enormous grins as they line up to welcome Pam

> *Pam enters, looking vaguely like our celebrity, in a vulgar sequinned gown, matching handbag, high heels, and far too many coatings of thick, smudged make-up. She is so terrified that she is visibly quaking and can hardly walk. Any part of her body that isn't wobbling is frozen rigid*

Long pause

Theresa (*gentle but unconvincing*) You ... look—terrific... Doesn't she, everyone?

Sharon Just like the real thing.

Jackie Very good. Yes...

Another pause

Theresa Mum? Mum? How do you feel? Can you speak? She's lost her voice. (*She feels her*) She's frozen solid!

Betty Oh, Pam, this is no good—look at you, you're petrified.

Theresa She'll be fine. Once she hears the applause. Doctor Footlights will sort her out. Won't he, Mum?

Pam remains rigid and silent

Sharon Perhaps we should try singing a few lines.

Sharon leads Pam C and stands her by the microphone

> Off you go, then. Pam?

Pam breaks down into tears. Sharon comforts her

> First night nerves...

Betty Come on, that's enough of all this. We'll have to cancel.

Theresa No! No! She'll be all right. She really will! Nan, fetch the gin. Jackie, buy some Prozac. And Sharon, sort the wig out; she looks like she's just had an electric shock.

Sharon Right!

Betty and Jackie run off in one direction, Sharon in the other. Just after exiting, Sharon rushes on again. She grabs the wig off the head of the frozen Pam and exits with it

Pam grabs at her hairnet and looks even more panicked. Theresa assists her back to the dressing-room as the Lights fade to Black-out

Music: instrumental versions of There's No Business Like Show Business

SCENE 3

When the Lights come up on stage they are a wash of colour. We are watching the concert

Betty and Sharon are on stage with the bingo ball machine seen in Act I. Sharon is in a glitzy vulgar dress with two "prizes" at her feet—a bottle of champagne and a large box of chocolates. Betty, in her kiss-me-quick hat and crew sweatshirt, is calling out the bingo numbers with the aid of a hand-held microphone

Betty The next prize in the raffle goes to number… (*She reaches into the machine*) Hang on, I can't get my hand on a ball. Bugger! (*She gets a ball*) Here you go. Number— (*she squints*) twelve. Number twelve is the winner! Come and get your prize!

The sound of an audience applauding and an electronic fanfare. Sharon takes the box of chocolates and hands them to someone just off stage, with a cheery smile. We see the be-suited hand reaching on to the stage to take the prize

Next number up, then! Let's have your eyes down for a full house … not that you get a full house in this, 'cos it's just a raffle. And later on—we got a celebrity raffle; a big star raffle, so stay tuned! Or stay sat, looking at the stage, whatever. Now then, next prize goes to— (*she selects a ball*) number nine! Number nine! Come and get your prize—number nine!

Applause and fanfare. Sharon takes the champagne to the wings, ready to pass over the prize. Betty re-examines the ball

No, hang on—go and sit down again.

A look from Sharon

I read it the wrong way round. Stupid machine gave it me upside down. Number six is the winner. Lucky six the winner!

Applause and fanfare. Sharon hands the champagne over, another set of hands reaching out for the prize. Betty, meanwhile, selects another ball

And our final prize, the final number is—seventeen! Who's got that one, then? Yes, seventeen! There's our winner, a prize for our final winner!

Applause and fanfare. Sharon looks around in a panic because there are no prizes left. Desperately, she pulls back the curtain and grabs the urn from the corner of the stage. She hands it into the wings as a prize. A final fanfare

Betty takes a bow before exiting with the microphone in her hand

Sharon glances into the audience with great concern, then follows Betty off

Applause from the audience

Theresa walks on stage for her role as the compere, dressed in a tuxedo

She crosses to the microphone stand. A spotlight picks her out. She starts talking, but the audience cannot hear anything she says

After a few moments, Betty creeps on stage with the missing microphone in her hand. She enters in a low awkward stoop, presuming a lack of height will make her less conspicuous

She gives the microphone to Theresa, who starts again. She is extremely nervous

Theresa Thank you very much to Betty there, one of our management team at the Pleasure Pier. And Sharon will be joining up soon—us soon, again—later—as we welcome our special guest star for this evening's entertaining—ment.

Jackie enters in a sequinned dress and high heels, accompanied by Sharon

They proceed to noisily drag the bingo ball machine off stage. Theresa quickly lends a hand

They go off

Theresa returns to the microphone

I must also take this opportune to thank our wonderful magicians for their adorable fire-eating rabbit routines—(*she checks her notes*) fire eating and adorable rabbit routines. Thanks too to Princess Dance Academy for that delightful excerpt from *Swine Lake*. And that rounds off all but our final, last finale evening ... of our ending. (*She looks at a piece of note paper from her pocket and then starts again, with renewed determination to get it right*) To end our evening, we are very especially pleased to welcome a true stare in anyone's book. The Pleasure Pier is thrilled and delighted to welcome, the one and only—Miss ... [CELEBRITY].

A huge burst of applause. A big proud smile from Theresa

Black-out

Two spotlights rise at either side of the stage, revealing Sharon and Jackie, gesturing enthusiastically towards c. *We can make out a third figure in the darkness* c

A musical introduction plays amidst loud, thundering applause. The music ends and the applause quietens. Jackie and Sharon turn to face c. *We hear the opening bars of a big band backing track of the forthcoming song. The two spotlights slowly fade out. At the moment just before the first vocal line of the song, the centre spotlight flashes on*

The figure turns to face front. We see Pam, all dressed up, open-mouthed and rigid with fear. She utters not one word as the music continues through the song. After a few moments, the Lights snap cross-fade to the two side spotlights, revealing a very shocked Sharon and Jackie. They stare, embarrassed, at the audience. Realizing they must cover for the situation, they begin to dance to the music. After a few moments, the Lights then cross-fade back to the centre spotlight, catching Pam just as she begins to violently vomit into her matching handbag. Sharon edges into the spotlight and puts her arm around Pam. She signals to cut the music, which grinds and thuds to a halt. The sound of the audience murmuring loudly, plus the odd whistle of disapproval. Full Lights rise on stage

Sharon walks Pam into the wings, followed by Jackie

Betty and Theresa enter from opposite sides. Betty hands a microphone to Theresa, then quickly exits

Theresa holds the microphone to her mouth. She thinks for a moment. Suddenly, a big smile

Thank you, [CELEBRITY]!

The audience yell and boo loudly. Theresa panics. She holds her hands up to ask them to quieten, then nervously speaks again. The smile has gone

All right, all right. Erm—er, you see, we had… I'm sorry. I'm sorry, ladies and gentlemen. That was not in fact her at all. You may have realized that. It was… It was actually my mother.

Murmurs of disapproval in the audience

If I could just explain—you see—[CELEBRITY]—cancelled. She couldn't come. She had the flu. But we couldn't afford to cancel the show; we don't have the money. I know we could have waited and maybe she would have come later on, but we were so lucky to get this date in the first place, chances are she wouldn't have managed it. And we're surviving week to week as it is, we couldn't last any longer without the money from tonight. And we'd all put so much work in, and when we heard, we just… We had to try something. We thought if Mum got dressed up, she could sing a chorus or two, then say she had a frog in her throat and just do the raffle. But I don't think Mum can even manage the raffle; I think she'd be sick in the bucket. I'm really very sorry. If you come to the box office, I'll start giving your money back. And if you do want your money back, you can have it. But if you can afford not to, then… I know you must be angry and disappointed, but… Perhaps you could make it a donation. For the pier. That's the only reason we did this. We're only here for the pier! (*Her accidental joke has made herself laugh*) Sorry—I wasn't trying to be funny. I know this situation isn't funny. (*She laughs again*) It isn't funny at all. (*Her laughter becomes crying tears*)

Fade to Black-out. Sad music in the scene change

SCENE 4

The show over, the golden curtain has been half lowered to the floor

Sharon sits comforting a very distressed Pam, sat with her hair in a net and the wig removed. Sharon is wiping the make-up from Pam's face. Jackie and Betty also sit or stand close by

Sharon Come on, now, Pam. No point crying over spilt milk, as they say.

Pam What did I do?

Sharon It was nerves, that's all. Nothing to be ashamed of.

Pam I threw up in [CELEBRITY]'s handbag!

Jackie It wasn't her bag. It was from a shop. And it can be cleaned. Don't worry over silly things.

Pam I just couldn't do it. I don't know why—it's my age, I'm so insecure——

Sharon That's enough now——

Pam I just lost control all of a sudden, it was like I became possessed.

Sharon That was how it looked to me. I was waiting for your head to spin around.

Pam What a terrible night.

Jackie Oh, it wasn't that bad.

Pam What!?

Jackie The dancing and the magician both got lots of applause.

Betty And the bingo.

Jackie Yes—the bingo. That went down really well. And people left very happy with some lovely prizes.

Sharon And some unexpected prizes...

Pam Well, I just can't see how any of you can put a gloss on tonight. The moment when I stepped out on this stage was the death of this pier.

Sharon We don't know that yet.

Jackie That's right. Let's not jump to conclusions. We need to just wait and see how many asked for their money back.

Pam Wouldn't you ask for your money back after that fiasco?

Jackie No. No, I wouldn't.

Sharon And nor would I.

Betty I bloody would.

Jackie shoots a look at her

Well, let's be honest. What did they get for their twenty-five quid? Some bunch of fourteen-year-olds clomping about in tights and Pam bringing up her dinner. I won't lie to you, Pam. If it was me, I'd have got back me money. But people are different. I'm not saying everyone is like that. I just wouldn't be too hopeful. What's important in all this is that you don't blame yourself——

Jackie That's right.

Betty We were all of us in this together. We all run this pier, we all put on this show.

Jackie Yes.

Betty We were all on stage. We were all in the gamble.

Jackie Yes.

Betty We were all out there with you.

Sharon Yeah, all of us.

Jackie Right.

Betty We all stood behind that microphone, we all lost our nerve, we all coughed up lasagne——

Sharon Yes, all right, Betty, I think we've got the general idea now.

Jackie We mustn't ever forget that we're a team. And we are. A good team. Whether this is the end or not, we still got this far. So we must be a good team... And I'm proud of what you tried to do tonight, Pam. It took real guts. And for all our differences; I admire that.

Silence

And you should take off that hairnet, you look like an inmate at Bedlam.

Jackie removes the hairnet from Pam's head

Theresa enters, carrying a cash box and some sheets of paper

Sharon What's the news, then?

Theresa Good and bad, really. About seventy per cent wanted refunds. But that left us with enough to cover our costs, so we haven't really lost anything.

Pam But how long can we survive on what there is?

Theresa I think we should be optimistic.

Pam Why?

Theresa We have enough to pay for a few minor things——

Pam Well, that's hardly——

Theresa And a little left over to let us open sections of the pier.

Sharon What sections exactly?

Theresa The Hall of Mirrors. The Bingo.

Sharon And?

Theresa I don't know; Andy Pandy's Merry-Go-Round?

Sharon No—still lethal.

Theresa But even if we only start up the Bingo, that will bring something in.

Betty Not a lot, dear.

Theresa Don't forget we still have Sharon's aerobic money. If we can just survive ourselves, we can still get more done.

Jackie It's just not right, though, is it? Why should all this have to be done privately. A pier isn't a business entity, it's part of the history of the place, it's heritage. The council will quite happily give money to some two hundred year old house just because some Lord used to live there, but there's more lifetimes, more drama and joy has walked along these planks than some old cottage. It makes me angry. Why haven't the council helped us out? They haven't even lifted a finger. I don't know how they judge these things. They discover Charles Dickens stopped for a sandwich at some old shop, and a century later they give it a grant and call it the Charles Dickens Snackplace Heritage Centre. And we have all this, all these decades, all this life—and nothing. They don't even visit. Where were they tonight? Where was the council? Where was the Mayor? Where was the heritage department? That's what I want to know!

Theresa Row D, seats eleven to twenty.

Pam You are joking!

Theresa I'm not. They introduced themselves when they asked for their money back.

Pam stands up

Pam That's it! That's it! There's nothing more we can do. Can we please just bring an end to this nightmare now.

Theresa Nightmare?

Pam Yes! Nightmare.

Theresa Look, Mum, I know tonight was horrible for everyone, but otherwise it's all been getting so much better. I know we've had difficulties, but I realized months ago that you and Jackie were just never going to——

Pam Jackie? What do you mean, Jackie? I'm not talking about her. (*To Jackie*) I'm not, really. I wasn't saying you were the nightmare. You're not a nightmare, Jackie.

Jackie Thank you.

Pam I wasn't saying... (*To Theresa*) Jackie's actually been rather supportive tonight, actually, so—so you can stop harping on about me and Jackie for five minutes.

Theresa I wasn't harping on anything——

Pam You were, you were. You've turned it all into such a big drama, I can't help feeling you were more bothered about it than I ever was.

Theresa Well, I'm sorry if I——

Pam There's nothing to be sorry about; I'm just saying. I think we're all adult enough to look forward. I've been through enough tonight to know what real distress is. And it is not our differences. So is that clear now?

Theresa Yes, perfectly. And I'm very pleased to hear you say that. It's wonderful.

Pam It's not wonderful——

Theresa No, it is. It is wonderful. My mother and my step-mother don't hate each other any more.

Pam I never hated her.

Betty Yes, you did!

Pam Not now, Betty.

Betty You said just last week she looked like a tart with a——

Pam Nan, don't! Stop putting words into my mouth.

Betty Putting words into your mouth? I wouldn't have thought there was room with all those fillings.

Pam Why are you having a go at me now? Haven't I suffered enough humiliation tonight?

Theresa All right, everyone calm down. We don't need to discuss this now. Everyone is a bit on edge. So let's get some fresh air, lock up, and meet again on Monday.

Sharon That's a good idea, I think she's right. Let's just get home and take our minds off it. Have a bit of sex.

Betty Chance would be a fine thing.

Theresa Where is Stevey anyway?

Sharon Taking the seal back.

Theresa Oh. Well, that's good.

Sharon Come on, Theresa. I'll help you start locking up.

Theresa Is everyone OK with that? We'll talk Monday?

Jackie I think that's best.

Sharon Come with me, Betty, you've still got all the keys.

Betty Right you are, dear.

Sharon and Betty exit

Theresa (*to Pam*) I'll drop you home, shall I? You shouldn't drive really.

Pam You might be right.

Theresa I'm so sorry about tonight, Mum. (*She kisses Pam on the cheek*) It'll all come right in the end. (*She begins to walk off*)

Pam Theresa?

Theresa stops and turns

I'm not coming back here on Monday.

Theresa Tuesday, then.

Pam No. I'm finished with this place now. It's killing me.

Theresa Mum, please——

Pam Theresa. (*Gently*) I never really belonged. And it's all been too much. I just want a simple life. A nice job in a supermarket, *Blind Date* on a Saturday. And just keeping the house in one piece. Cockles, turnstiles and ghost trains I can live without. I've put in what I can. And now you can let me go. And it'll be better for it.

Theresa No, it won't. You're part of this. It's what Dad wanted.

Pam Your father did not want me here to contribute to the life of the bloody
pier. He put me in this situation so that I'd have to work with Jackie. So I
couldn't avoid her. He wanted me to suffer her company day in and day
out. And you know why?

Theresa No.

Pam So that eventually I would get used to her. So that eventually I would
run out of insults. So that eventually I could see why he loved her... So I
could see that he simply didn't love me... And that it isn't her fault. (*She
looks at Jackie, giving her a brave smile*) That's why I was here on the pier.
And that's why I don't need to be here anymore. (*She walks to Theresa and
gives her a kiss*) I'll wait for you near the car.

Pam walks off

Theresa is very emotional. Jackie crosses to her and gives her a big hug

The Lights fade to Black-out

SCENE 5

Music. Spotlight on a sign that reads "Monday"

*The gold curtain has been cleared and is replaced by a black curtain which
is able to separate. The Lights come up, revealing the empty stage of the pier
theatre. A rusty ride car from the ghost train is* c

Theresa is sitting in it

Sharon enters

Sharon What are you doing here? I've been looking everywhere.

Theresa Just fancied a bit of solitude.

Sharon And you decided to spend it sitting in a rusty old pram?

Theresa It's not a pram. It's one of the cars from the ghost train.

Sharon What's it doing in the theatre?

Theresa It was in the store room, near where we put the curtain.

Sharon Just the one, is there?

Theresa Yes, but there's room for two people in here.

Sharon You want me to sit with you in a rusty ride car? That's going
absolutely nowhere? This has all hit you worse than I thought.

Theresa I just saw it there and wanted to wheel it out straight away. I gave
it a good dusting down, but it still looks a bit sorry for itself.

Sharon I should say so.

Theresa Brings back memories, though. I used to love that old ghost train.

Sharon Yes, I remember you saying... Look, I was going to pop down the pub and have a quick pint, I thought you might like to come.

Theresa I wouldn't make very good company today.

Sharon Of course you would, don't be daft.

Theresa I'll just stay here, thanks.

Sharon Theresa, I know you're disappointed. But the decision had to be made. We all came to meet this morning with an open mind, and we're all doing what we think is best.

Theresa I know that, I know. But there was still hope, I thought. The application for lottery money was already done. Why not just wait and see?

Sharon We would never match the money. How can we raise hundreds of thousands of pounds? We spent the last month trying to raise just ten thousand, and all we ended up with was fifty quid and a court summons.

Theresa I know you're right. I just... It's still difficult to get my head around it.

Sharon That's why you need a pint inside you. A glass of Theakston's Extra Strong Old Peculiar and everything will look very different. Two glasses and it won't even be in focus! Besides, it's not like we're knocking the pier down or anything. Somebody really caring might buy it, bring it back to its former glory.

Theresa Or turn it into a car park.

Sharon Don't go miserable on me, Theresa, or I'll call in Stevey to sort you out.

Theresa I must speak to him later. He seemed quite upset.

Sharon He is a bit disappointed. He was enjoying himself down here. Still, he's been down the Sealife Centre to see if they might have a job for him.

Theresa As a security guard?

Sharon As a grey seal. Well, he knows the costume fits. He also had this idea of doing donkey rides on the beach. But when you think about it, it's a bit cruel, isn't it? A bit old-fashioned.

Theresa I don't think it would do very well.

Sharon That's what I said.

Theresa I don't know what would do well at the seafront these days. People just go abroad. The only people to come here now are pensioners. And half of them fall asleep as soon as they're sat down.

Sharon Give it a bit of time. You'll see, something always gets done at the last minute. That's how this country works. We watch things decline and rust and crumble for years, and pay no attention. Then just as it's about to break in two and smash to pieces, everyone leaps up and says we have to save it—piers, theatres, stately homes; you name it... See, you're getting me all cynical and depressed now. Thanks a bunch!

Theresa Do you want to sit in the car?

Sharon Oh, go on, then. (*She climbs into the ride car and sits next to Theresa*)

Theresa How does it feel?

Sharon Nice. A little weird—but nice.

Jackie enters

Jackie You won't get very far in that.

Theresa Hi.

Jackie Been quite a day, hasn't it. I feel terribly guilty, I hope you don't feel I've let you down.

Theresa No, not at all. I understand how everyone feels, completely. To work for all these months with no money was hard on everyone.

Jackie It was just the prospect of it carrying on like this, all the stress. It was such an uphill struggle.

Theresa It was.

Jackie But something good will come of it. Some fabulous American will buy the place and really look after it; and we'll all make lots of money from the sale and—I don't know—maybe buy back a section of it.

Sharon Yes, we could run the Hot Doughnut parlour.

Jackie Whatever happens, you'll see it was the right decision.

Theresa I just can't help feeling that I've let my father down.

Jackie Oh, Theresa...

Theresa I'm just sad for him. The pier is going to be closed up again. He went to all that effort with his will to give the place a chance. And here we are. At the end of the day, whether it was the right decision for all of us or not; Dad didn't get what he wanted.

Jackie But he brought all of us together, like a family. The five people he loved most in the world worked here as a team, as friends... I spoke to Pam for forty minutes when I rang her about the decision this morning. Forty minutes and not a single cross word or sharp remark. That's thirty-nine minutes and forty seconds longer than ever before. It was like we were different people... So maybe your father got what he wanted after all. Not the pier, maybe; but what he really wanted. That's how I like to look at it. And I think you should try and see that too. OK?

Theresa Yeah.

Sharon We'll be going down the pub in a minute, if you want to come?

Jackie That would be great.

Sharon And bring Betty.

Jackie She's already there. She got to know one of the local technicians who helped with the show.

Theresa Nan's out drinking with a technician? At her age?

Sharon Why not? You should try and get one yourself, do you the power of good.

Theresa I'm not looking for romance right now, thank you.

Sharon Believe me, love, you'll get no romance from a technician! It'll be over before you've put your Mills and Boon down.

Jackie laughs

Jackie Well, if I'm going to join you, I better get a few more things done.

Sharon Anything we can help with?

Jackie Well, yes—the main thing is Michael's ashes. I know they're here somewhere, but I can't find them for the life of me.

Sharon His ashes?

Jackie Yes. In the urn. Have you seen them?

Sharon Erm… Not since the show…

Jackie I'll check the store room again.

Sharon Good idea.

Jackie exits

Sharon eases herself out of the ride car

Theresa Something the matter?

Sharon I just need to go and make a few urgent phone calls. See you at the pub.

Sharon takes a few casual steps, then runs off into the wings

Theresa sits alone in the ride car for a moment. Lights close in around her until she is lit only by a small pool of light. Quiet and distant at first, then building in volume—we hear the noises of a funfair ghost train running along its track. We hear the clicking noises, the mechanical screams and whistles, the sounds of the ride car crashing through wooden flapping doors and down curved ramps. Amidst all the noise, Theresa smiles and hugs herself tightly. The ride car then slowly turns (as if by magic) to face upstage. The black curtain separates to reveal a ghost train kaleidoscope effect: reducing spirals of red light bulbs, spinning round and round to give a hypnotic image. The ride car moves across the stage and towards the kaleidoscope, with the noises continuing. As it reaches the kaleidoscope, the stage Lights fade to Black-out, then the red bulbs also fade out as the sound effects dim to silence

CURTAIN

FURNITURE AND PROPERTY LIST

Further dressing may be added at the director's discretion

ACT I

SCENE 1

On stage: Basic tables
Chairs
Filing cabinets
Broken deck-chair
Theatre poster
Boxes
Crates
Turntable
Speakers
Stacks of seven inch records
Tatty sign for pier's radio station
Litter
Dust
Old book
Electrical socket

Off stage: Bags of shopping containing packets of biscuits, two stacks of Max Pax instant cup drinks, kettle, 2 plates, plastic bottle of water (**Theresa**)

Personal: **Sharon:** bar of chocolate

SCENE 2

Strike: Boxes
Litter
Dust
Bags of shopping

Set: "Two Days Later" sign
Rusty automated bingo machine containing balls

Off stage: Large cardboard box containing giant fur body costume and massive teddy bear head (**Jackie**)

Personal: **Jackie:** receipts

Scene 3

Strike: "Two Days Later" sign

Set: "Later That Day" sign
Stacks of pastel-coloured paint pots
Paint brushes
Cup of water
Glass
Water bottle

Off stage: **Jackie**'s receipts (**Pam**)
Clipboard (**Theresa**)

Personal: **Jackie:** tissue

Scene 4

On stage: "The Next Morning" sign
Towels

Personal: **Pam:** old leg warmers, headband

Scene 5

On stage: "Another Month Later" sign

Personal: **Jackie:** "Save Our Pier" sandwich boards

Scene 6

On stage: Pier railings
Strings of coloured light bulbs
Row of deck-chairs
Sign displaying spooky figure pointing to ghost train
Betty's needlework
2 sections of advertising banner stitched together wrongly
Box of coloured bulbs
Cleaning cloth

Off stage: Fax machine with letter hanging out of it (**Betty**)

Personal: **Betty:** kiss-me-quick hat
               Sharon: candyfloss

SCENE 7

On stage: As before

Off stage: Clipboard (**Betty**)
               Funeral urn (**Jackie**)

Personal: **Sharon:** rubber ring with swan head, flippers, red nose
               Theresa: 2 Punch and Judy puppets

ACT II

SCENE 1

On stage: "Three Months Later" sign
               Shimmering golden curtain backdrop

Off stage: Microphone on stand (**Jackie**)
               Clipboard (**Pam**)
               Clipboard, pot of seafood (**Betty**)

Personal: **Betty:** bunch of keys, mobile phone

SCENE 2

Strike: "Three Months Later" sign

Set: "One Hour to Show Time" sign
               Microphone

Off stage: Reel of cable (**Betty**)
               Funereal urn (**Jackie**)
               Handbag (**Pam**)

Personal: **Sharon:** apron covered in make-up smudges
               Betty: clipboard, headphones
               Pam: hairnet, wig

SCENE 3

Strike: "One Hour to Show Time" sign

Set: Bingo ball machine
              Bottle of champagne
              Large box of chocolates
              Hand-held microphone

Off stage: Microphone (**Betty**)
              Handbag (**Pam**)

Personal: **Betty**: kiss-me-quick hat
              Theresa: notes, piece of note paper

SCENE 4

Set: **Sharon**'s make-up things
              Pam's wig

Off stage: Cash box, sheets of paper (**Theresa**)

Personal: **Pam:** hairnet

SCENE 5

Set: "Monday" sign
              Black curtain

Strike: Gold curtain
              Rusty ride car from the ghost train

LIGHTING PLOT

Property fittings required: coloured bulbs
Various settings

ACT I, SCENE 1

To open: Darkness

Cue 1 Music fades (Page 1)
Very slowly bring up lights

Cue 2 **Pam** stares at **Sharon** (Page 12)
Black-out

ACT I, SCENE 2

To open: Spotlight on banner; morning lighting when ready

Cue 3 **Betty** looks teddy bear in the eye (Page 17)
Black-out

ACT I, SCENE 3

To open: Spotlight on banner; lights up on **Sharon** and **Jackie** when ready

Cue 4 **Theresa** looks down at her clothes (Page 24)
Black-out

ACT I, SCENE 4

To open: Spotlight on banner, then general lighting

Cue 5 **Sharon**: "Now for the real action!" (Page 27)
Snap black-out

Cue 6   Music starts up   (Page 27)
              Spotlight on banner, then cross-fade to office

Cue 7   Music climaxes   (Page 27)
              Snap black-out

ACT I, Scene 5

To open: Darkness

Cue 8   Set is cleared for Scene 6   (Page 27)
              Spotlight on banner

ACT I, Scene 6

To open: Clear, sunny day lighting

Cue 9   Music   (Page 33)
              Black-out

ACT I, Scene 7

To open: Overall general lighting

Cue 10   **Theresa**: "I know, but it's a step forward, isn't it?"   (Page 36)
              Slowly fade lights to black-out

ACT II, Scene 1

To open: Spotlight on banner; then theatre lighting on stage

Cue 11   **Theresa**: "We don't have time for this!"   (Page 38)
              Black-out

Cue 12   **Theresa**: "Stevey?"   (Page 38)
              Spotlight c

Cue 13   Music stops   (Page 38)
              Return lights to normal

Cue 14   **Pam**: "So get to it!"   (Page 45)
             Black-out

ACT II, Scene 2

To open: Spotlight on banner; then theatre lighting

Cue 15   **Theresa** escorts **Pam** off   (Page 48)
             Fade lights to black-out

ACT II, Scene 3

To open: Colourful theatre lighting

Cue 16   **Theresa** crosses to microphone   (Page 49)
             Spotlight on **Theresa**

Cue 17   **Theresa** smiles at huge burst of applause   (Page 50)
             Black-out; then spotlights on both sides of stage

Cue 18   Opening bars of big band backing track   (Page 50)
             Slowly fade out spotlights; then just before first vocal
             line of song, flash on spotlight C

Cue 19   **Pam** stands rigid   (Page 50)
             Snap cross-fade to two side spotlights

Cue 20   **Sharon** and **Jackie** dance   (Page 50)
             Cross-fade to spotlight C

Cue 21   Sound of audience murmurs and whistles   (Page 50)
             Bring up full lighting on stage

Cue 22   **Theresa** starts to cry   (Page 51)
             Fade lights to black-out

ACT II, Scene 4

To open: Overall theatre lighting on stage

Cue 23   **Jackie** hugs **Theresa**   (Page 56)
             Fade lights to black-out

ACT II, SCENE 5

To open: Spotlight on banner; then general theatre lighting

Cue 24   **Sharon** runs off   (Page 59)
             After a moment, reduce lighting to small pool of light
                on **Theresa**

Cue 25   Curtain separates   (Page 59)
             Ghost train kaleidoscope effect: reducing circles of
                red light bulbs, spinning round and round

Cue 26   Ride car reaches kaleidoscope   (Page 59)
             Fade stage lights to black-out, then red bulbs also

EFFECTS PLOT

ACT I

Cue 10	Black-out	(Page 24)
	Music: aerobics tape—heavy beat, pop music, continuing	
Cue 11	**Pam** turns music volume down	(Page 25)
	Fade down music	
Cue 12	**Sharon** turns music volume up high	(Page 25)
	Increase music volume	
Cue 13	**Sharon** turns off music	(Page 26)
	Cut music	
Cue 14	Snap black-out	(Page 27)
	Music: Hooked on Classics, *or another piece if preferred*	
Cue 15	**All** hit a dynamic final pose	(Page 27)
	Music climaxes	
Cue 16	To open Scene 5	(Page 27)
	Music	
Cue 17	To open Scene 6	(Page 27)
	Background noises of sea and birds	
Cue 18	**Sharon** and **Betty** look out to sea	(Page 28)
	Sound of seagull flying past	
Cue 19	**Theresa** is about to exit	(Page 32)
	Sound of explosion	
Cue 20	**Betty** and **Theresa** exit	(Page 33)
	Music	

ACT II

Cue 21	**Jackie**: "…seems to make him happy."	(Page 38)
	Loud screech from stage speakers	
Cue 22	**Theresa**: "This is silly, he can't hear me."	(Page 38)
	Music of the backing track blasting through speakers	
Cue 23	**Pam**, **Jackie** and **Theresa** dance for a few moments	(Page 38)
	Cut music	

Cue 24	**Theresa**: "Anything else Jackie needs to buy?" *Mobile phone rings, continuing*	(Page 41)
Cue 25	**Pam** answers the mobile phone *Cut ringing*	(Page 41)
Cue 26	Black-out *Instrumental big band music, continuing*	(Page 45)
Cue 27	**Theresa** starts speaking *Fade music*	(Page 46)
Cue 28	Black-out *Music: instrumental versions of* There's No Business Like Show Business	(Page 48)
Cue 29	**Betty**: "Come and get your prize!" *The sound of audience applauding and electronic fanfare*	(Page 48)
Cue 30	**Betty**: "Come and get your prize—number nine!" *Applause and fanfare*	(Page 48)
Cue 31	**Betty**: "Lucky six the winner!" *Applause and fanfare*	(Page 49)
Cue 32	**Betty**: "…prize for our final winner!" *Applause and fanfare*	(Page 49)
Cue 33	**Sharon** hands over urn *Fanfare*	(Page 49)
Cue 34	**Sharon** exits *Applause from audience*	(Page 49)
Cue 35	**Theresa**: "…the one and only—Miss … [CELEBRITY]." *Huge burst of applause*	(Page 50)
Cue 36	Spotlights come up *Musical introduction amidst loud, thundering applause,* *then end music and fade applause*	(Page 50)
Cue 37	**Jackie** and **Sharon** turn to face C *Play opening bars of big band backing track of the* *forthcoming song*	(Page 50)

Cue 38	**Sharon** signals to cut music *Music grinds and thuds to a halt; sound of audience murmuring loudly, and the odd whistle of disapproval*	(Page 50)
Cue 39	**Theresa**: "Thank you, [CELEBRITY]!" *Sound of audience yelling and booing loudly*	(Page 51)
Cue 40	**Theresa**: "It was actually my mother." *Sounds of disapproving murmurs from audience*	(Page 51)
Cue 41	Black-out *Sad music during scene change*	(Page 51)
Cue 42	To open Scene 5 *Music*	(Page 56)
Cue 43	**Theresa** is lit by small pool of light *Quiet and distant at first, then building in volume: noises of fun fair ghost train running along its track; clicking noises, mechanical screams and whistles, sounds of ride car crashing through wooden flapping doors and down curved ramps, continuing*	(Page 59)
Cue 44	Lights and red bulbs fade out *Fade out sound effects*	(Page 59)